The Tudor monarchies, 1485–1603

John McGurk

CAMBRIDGE
UNIVERSITY PRESS

PUBLISHED BY THE PRESS SYNDICATE OF THE UNIVERSITY OF CAMBRIDGE
The Pitt Building, Trumpington Street, Cambridge, United Kingdom

CAMBRIDGE UNIVERSITY PRESS
The Edinburgh Building, Cambridge CB2 2RU, UK
40 West 20th Street, New York, NY 10011–4211, USA
477 Williamstown Road, Port Melbourne, VIC 3207, Australia
Ruiz de Alarcón 13, 28014 Madrid, Spain
Dock House, The Waterfront, Cape Town 8001, South Africa

http://www.cambridge.org

First published 1999
Third printing 2002

Printed in the United Kingdom at the University Press, Cambridge

Typeset in Tiepolo and Formata

A catalogue record for this book is avaiable from the British Library

ISBN 0 521 59665 3 paperback

Text design by Newton Harris Design Partnership

ACKNOWLEDGEMENTS
Cover, by courtesy of the National Portrait Gallery, London; 22, Christie's
Images, Bridgeman Art Library, London/New York; 32, Philip Mould, Historical
Portraits Ltd, London, Bridgeman Art Library, London/New York; 38, The
Trustees of the Weston Park Foundation, Bridgeman Art Library, London/New
York; 65, Sudeley Castle, Gloucestershire, Bridgeman Art Library, London/New
York; 79, Private collection, The Bridgeman Art Library, London/New York; 92,
Private collection, The Bridgeman Art Library, London/New York; 98, Fotomas
Index; 100, Private collection, The Bridgeman Art Library, London/New York

The cover illustration is an allegorical painting of about 1548, showing popery
and superstition being overthrown by Henry VIII and his son, Edward VI, and
the pure Word of God being substituted in their place. Henry VIII is seen on his
death bed, gesturing to his son Edward VI. On Edward's left, are members of the
Regency Council: Edward Seymour, John Dudley, Thomas Cranmer and John
Russell. The pope is shown being crushed by the new Prayer Book.

Contents

1 The monarchy   **1**

The monarch and the law   1
The rise of bureaucracy   3
The monarch in parliament   6
Document case study   *8*

2 York and Lancaster: the background to the Tudors   **14**

The Wars of the Roses   14
The Yorkist ascendancy   15
Edward IV   16
Richard III   17
Document case study   *19*

3 Henry VII: 1485–1509   **22**

The foundation of the Tudor dynasty   23
Henry VII: his character and abilities   23
Henry's administration: law and order and finance   24
Henry VII and Wales   25
The Council of the North   26
Foreign affairs   26
Henry VII and Ireland   27
Henry's achievements   29
Document case study   *29*

4 Henry VIII: 1509–1547   **32**

The character of Henry VIII   33
Renaissance England   33
Cardinal Wolsey   34
Foreign policy: Wolsey and the king   35
The royal supremacy and the Reformation   37
Henry VIII's last years   41
Henry VIII and Wales   41
Henry VIII and Ireland   42
Henry VIII and the kingdom of Scotland   44
Document case study   *46*

Contents

5 Edward VI: 1547–1553   **49**

Somerset: Protector of the Realm, 1547–1549   49
Financial problems   50
Religious change   50
Social policy and rebellion   51
The rule of Northumberland, 1549–1553   53
Document case study   *55*

6 Mary Tudor: 1553–1558   **59**

The accession and early legislation   59
The religious settlement   61
The Spanish marriage   61
The Wyatt Rebellion   62
The Catholic restoration   63
Mary's last years   64
Document case study   *66*

7 Elizabeth I: the early years, 1558–1588   **70**

An insecure accession   70
The problem of religion   71
The Elizabethan settlement   72
Puritan opposition   73
The Catholic threat   74
The Northern Rebellion, 1569   75
Catholic martyrs   77
The international scene   78
The execution of Mary Queen of Scots   81
Document case study   *81*

8 Elizabeth I: the later years, 1588–1603   **87**

The Armada   87
The economy   88
Parliament, puritans and opposition to the queen   90
Local government and administration   95
The cult of Gloriana and the Elizabethan Age   98
Document case study   *101*

Conclusion   **106**

Select bibliography   112
Chronology   117
Index   122

1

The monarchy

In Western European history, during the fifteenth and sixteenth centuries, the most important institution in political and constitutional change was the monarchy. Throughout the Middle Ages, royal power gradually strengthened until the normal position of the monarch was set at the apex of earthly power. Everywhere, kings and princes (and occasionally queens) became the instruments of law, order, security and prosperity. They offered their subjects protection, justice and a sense of political unity in return for their obedience, loyalty, support in war and in peace, and their support in the shape of personal service and taxation.

As royal power expanded, so too did bureaucracy. This meant that a series of checks on the absolute power[1] of the monarch began to emerge, making the machinery of government gradually more complex, and replacing mere personal rule. In time, the council, not the monarch, became the centre of power and government.

How quickly this change occurred in any one country depended on the prevailing conditions. Absolutism did not just disappear. Generally speaking, a belief in royal prerogatives and the pomp, majesty and 'divinity' of monarchs was enshrined in popular memory and emphasised by symbolic regalia and the ancient rites of the coronation. It was often, therefore, able to survive all manner of constitutional and violent revolutions.

The English monarchy was no exception. Monarchs succeeded by hereditary right and by election: hereditary right needed only to be based on royal blood, and election could simply be by acclamation. As a person apart, the monarch was regarded as God's instrument. Shakespeare, for example, had Richard II declaim:

> Not all the water in the rough rude sea
> Can wash the balm from an anointed king;
> The breath of worldly men cannot depose
> The deputy elected by the Lord.[2]

The monarch and the law

Many constitutional historians, however, argue that, by the fourteenth century, a balance of rights and duties between monarchs and subjects had developed in England. This balance favoured the exercise of limited power rather than absolutism, and allowed for co-operation, and even partnership, in the way in which the community was subject to the monarch. The solemn and symbolic rites of the coronation provided a memorable expression of these ideas, for they reflected how a monarch is subject to God and the law, and should rule with the happy consent and co-operation of the people. This latter concept, that of a commonweal, a *res publica*, contained within itself some notions of limitations on royal power. All were bound by the common 'weal' or good, and all, including the ruler, had a duty to maintain it.

By the late Middle Ages, the lawyers no longer upheld the ancient Roman principle that what pleases the prince has the force of law, but many of the major writers on the law did concede that the monarch had wide emergency powers, including, for example, the power to raise forces in time of invasion or the threat of it. The monarch's primary duty was the safety of his subjects. Moreover, the monarch was not at liberty to set aside the rights of the subject. From the early Middle Ages, the church's teaching on tyrannicide, that it was lawful to kill a tyrant, was clear enough, although many lawyers believed that tyrants would be punished in the next life or, at least, that their punishment should be in the hands of the pope, the vicar of Christ.

Despite a steady growth in religious scepticism and secularism in the fifteenth century, and the rapid succession of monarchs in this period, the ancient, traditional view of a king *sub Deo et sub lege* (under God and the law) remained strong. John Wycliffe had argued in the fourteenth century that the king reflected in his office the *divinity* of Christ, while the pope reflected only Christ's *humanity*. The cult of the monarch, which peaked in the reigns of Elizabeth I and of Charles I, developed from this. Literature, art and architecture and developments in the court were consciously used, and abused, to add to the majesty of the monarchy.

It is true, however, that Sir John Fortescue, the most prominent political theorist of the fifteenth century, put forward a view of a limited monarchy in which supreme power was exercised only in conjunction with the people. This meant that the king could neither make laws without the people nor the people without the king; therefore, the king could not change the laws nor impose taxes without the subjects' consent. Constitutional historians, like S. B. Chrimes and B. Wilkinson would, however, point out that Fortescue's picture of the ideal constitutional, limited, parliamentary type monarchy was not always relevant to the practices of his day. Fortescue was hardly describing the facts of government before 1460, but was describing a tradition that was much abused in his day and in danger of being destroyed. He frequently remarked that king, Lords and Commons were all bound by the traditional laws of the land and by the law of nature. This principle was seen as a safeguard against absolutism and tyranny: the monarch received his powers from God to enable his subjects to enjoy their rights and property not to oppress them.

Political philosophers, theologians and constitutional lawyers have always defined principles, theorised on the nature of political power and described ideal forms of government. Their works help us to understand the conflicts of power such as those between the monarch and the magnates, and between the king and people, and how these conflicts determined, to some extent, constitutional developments in England.

In the great political conflicts of the thirteenth and fourteenth centuries, for example, the long-drawn-out clash of interests and political aims between the king and the barons were partially responsible for the emergent patterns of the state's institutions. It is also clear that such patterns resulted from more than personality clashes or greed and the desire for power; they were also the result of a clash of principles and ideals. There is no general agreement on what is meant by the common 'weal' or good. This means, therefore, that monarchs cannot be labelled 'good' or 'bad' depending upon how they square up to a supposed ideal constitution. Both monarchy and people were aggressive on different occasions, each seeking justice, but differing on what was justice. King and Commons often clashed over who was the true defender of the nation's liberties.

The rise of bureaucracy

As the nation state emerged as a territorial unity, the king's ministers were ceasing to be his personal servants and could be said (depending on the circumstances) to be more officials of the state. By the middle of the fifteenth century, the Lord Chancellor, for example, was no longer the king's domestic clerk as he had been when king, court and royal household were itinerant, constantly travelling throughout the realm. With the increasing complexity of government, the personal control of the monarch over affairs was gradually devolved into a system that gave direction of affairs into other hands. Such a development created problems because authority had to be devolved to the great officers of state, who had, at times, to interfere with the lives and property of the king's subjects, not always to the subjects' advantage. As bureaucracy grew, so too did the power of these officers, and those who became overkeen to promote the royal interest disturbed the balance of politics and promoted royal despotism. Furthermore, attempts by the Lords and Commons to control the great officers of the household appeared to be a challenge to the supremacy of the monarch – once bureaucracy gets out of control, it can, in the end, destroy the health of the political system it was originally created to maintain. It was, therefore, from out of the royal household that the great departments of state began to evolve.

The Chancery

The Chancery, or writing office, was responsible for issuing all manner of writs. Its head, the Lord Chancellor, presided over a hierarchy of clerks, headed in turn by the Keeper of the Rolls. The office settled in Westminster, and the Chancellor became a leading minister of the king. He was an important member, and often the president, of the king's council, and later expressed the king's wishes at the opening of parliament. The Chancellor was also the Keeper of the Great Seal. Any document, so sealed, became a formal expression of the royal will.

Throughout medieval English history, it is impossible to exaggerate the importance of the sealed writ, written in the vernacular, by which administration from the centre could expand into the far reaches of the kingdom and yet be kept under central authority. Writs covered all matters dealing with law and order, and the rights and duties of individuals and corporate groups. For example, the king could send a writ to the sheriff of any county ordering him to free a serf; have sea walls repaired; or have a person's goods or lands restored to them if they had been wrongfully seized. Sealed writs also made it possible to transfer authority from the king to his ministers and from them to local officials. The office of the King's Secretary who kept the Signet seal, and who was responsible for dealing with the king's letters, did not become crucially important until the reign of Henry VIII. In origin, however, the Secretary and his office stemmed from the Chancery.[3]

The Exchequer

The Exchequer also expanded, moving out from the court to become the office of finance. Its duties were to receive, store and pay out money and audit the accounts. Its work was also shared by the Chamber and the Wardrobe which looked after the needs of the king and his court. The medieval Exchequer accompanied the king on his travels and wars, and provided all the necessary monies. The Exchequer was headed by the Treasurer[4] and the barons of the Exchequer. All these important officers of state were *ex officio* members of the king's council. The more complex and costly government became, the more the functions, import- ance and organisation of the Exchequer expanded. New forms of taxation, ways and means of expanding royal revenues and of facilitating royal credit all came within the orbit of the Exchequer's officials. Take, for example, the obvious complexities involved in the collection of the new tax (the poll tax) in 1377. A poll tax of 4d (4 old pence) a head was approved in parliament and was to be paid by all lay persons over the age of fourteen together with a 1s (1 shilling) tax from the beneficed clergy and 4d from all other ecclesiastics. Managing the king's debts became a burdensome part of the Exchequer's work. Income tax was tried at least four or five times at the beginning of the fifteenth century and revived again in 1450 and 1472 but did not become permanent until the nineteenth century. Edward IV (1461–70; 1471–83) restored the crown to solvency without income tax but he used Forced Loans and Benevolences (forced gifts of money).

Edward IV and Richard III first began to use the Chamber rather than the Exchequer to handle their finances. It was a smaller and more flexible department of the household than the Exchequer, which could be slow and cumbersome. Under Henry VII, the work of the Chamber again increased at the expense of the Exchequer until, by the 1490s, it became the centre of royal finances. The Chamber now dealt with all revenue from crown lands, profits from justice, feudal dues and most other sources of income. In practice, the Treasurer of the Chamber became the chief financial officer of the crown.

The king's council

The essential function of the king's council was to advise the king on the exercise of royal power. It developed from the ancient *curia regis*, a general body of the king's advisers. By 1236, a sworn council of advisers had emerged. The direct loyalty of each sworn councillor was to the king; Henry III, for example, regarded them as his personal servants. By 1341, councillors swore to perform the king's business not simply to give advice about it, and in doing so they were to act for the good of the realm as well as of the king. Hence the personnel of this council was of the highest political importance.

As royal business expanded, it became no longer acceptable for the monarchs alone to choose the councillors. This was because there was a natural tendency for them to choose councillors from those closest to them, often relatives or favourites, rather than from among the greater nobility, who traditionally claimed the right to sit on the king's council. Moreover, monarchs could then demand loyalty to their own interests, rather than to those of the common 'weal'. The greater nobility, the magnates, had always claimed to be the 'natural advisers' of the monarch and often reminded the king that the business of the council was as much the concern of the community as well as of the king. These clashes of interests would very gradually, and only partially, be resolved by the emergence of parliament where the greater magnates would be in the House of Lords, then the most powerful part of parliament.

During the fourteenth century, the council began to lose some of its personal contact with the king, and its importance within parliament also decreased; nevertheless, the council expanded its independent judicial activities by which it enforced the law. These activities continued into the fifteenth century and became influenced both by the weakness of royal authority when monarchs were under the age of majority and by the increasing self-importance of great lords, especially those of royal blood. The growing political power of the nobility helped to lay the foundations for the special sessions of the council, known later as the Council in the Marches of Wales, the Council of the North and the Star Chamber. The old advisory body, next to the monarch's side, would continue as the privy council; but there was hardly any corporate unity to this body until Thomas Cromwell's time. Even as early as 1406, however, it was assumed that some of the special councillors to be appointed in the parliament by the king or his advisers would remain 'about the king's person'. The bishop of Salisbury, in 1461, described himself in terms suitable to a privy councillor and, in 1469, Warwick and Clarence asserted that the king 'estranged the true lords of his blood from his secret council'. The famous organ of royal government, the privy council, which centralised royal control over the nation under the Tudors, was already emerging as an arm of government in the fifteenth century, and its advent disliked and opposed.

The king's council was, next to parliament, an important focus of politics. In the many proposals for the reform of the council in the fourteenth century the importance of its functions and personnel are clear. Hence, in a Commons petition of the late fourteenth century, the cry was for 'councillors who should understand their own function, their loyalty to the crown, to the parliament, and to each other'. Ideally they should be disinterested, diligent, free from faction, secrecy and have discretion – in other words, they should show solidarity in the interests of king, the nation and in their own. It is, therefore, impossible to put the work of the king's council into a formula; but membership of it remained a rich prize for successful politicians.

The Yorkist dynasty was pre-occupied with council reform. Edward IV did his best to make his council once more the instrument of the king, not of the magnates. In that sense he, too, laid the foundations for Tudor rule and a new political order. This, however, would not solve the ever present problems of keeping a balance between liberty of the subject and the authority of the rulers in both church and state.

The monarch in parliament

Westminster had become the centre of government: medieval kings were buried in its Abbey; the Chancery, Exchequer, Privy Seal offices and the Courts of the King's Bench and Common Pleas were normally housed in Westminster Palace. Its Great Hall was the scene of state trials. Throughout the Middle Ages, the real effective power of the monarch varied: for example, Edward I (1274–1307) conquered Wales and Scotland but the power of his son Edward II (1307–27) was negligible and his person execrated. Edward III (1327–77), after a reign of fifty years, died honoured by all, but his successor Richard II (1377–99) suffered the same fate as Edward II. Repeated rebellions destroyed the health of the first Lancastrian, Henry IV (1399–1413), but his son, Henry V (1413–22), was probably the most popular of the medieval kings. Henry VI's kingship (1422–61; 1470–71) went unchallenged from his birth until his mature manhood. Subsequent generations tried to have him canonised as a saint of the church. In a real sense, royal rule depended on how much subjects put their faith in the 'natural law' that a king should exercise sovereignty; indeed on how far his writ should run throughout the land, even in the exempt liberties, the certain small areas within the country where, traditionally, the kings writ did not apply. The great nobles did not claim elaborate dynastic sovereignty over their regions, but emphasised their kinship with the king of England.

The issuing of the king's writ, summoning all the leading men of the realm to give advice and judgements in parliaments, in conjunction with the king's main officials, was an important means of ensuring that the royal will was being discharged locally. It is important to remember that parliaments were summoned by the monarch. Edward I developed procedures and precedents in his frequent summoning of representatives of the shires: the knights of the shire, the burgesses of the towns and the clergy. It was, therefore, standard practice that they were empowered to give advice and consent on behalf of their communities. The writ summoning elected representatives in 1295 became a model for the future; and, as representatives, they had the power to do whatever was ordained by 'common counsel' while their shires and boroughs were obliged to do whatever their representatives had accepted in parliament.

The links established between crown and community were strained by the frequent and arbitrary demands for money, supplies and services for foreign war. Edward I faced demands for safeguards. Edward II was forced to accept reforms. Edward III's recklessly oppressive taxation for war expenses hastened a series of parliamentary crises between 1339 and 1341 and provoked armed resistance to tax collectors. The Commons began to demand redress of grievances before granting taxes – in a word, no tax to be levied without parliamentary consent. But it must be stressed that the Commons or Lower House was not yet an independent power representative of the main political forces. The nobility and the higher clergy stood between Commons and king and, at times, threatened to overshadow both.

However, Lords and Commons began to exercise some control over the king's ministers. In 1340, they requested that they be elected in parliament and be answerable there for their offices. During the crises of 1376 to 1388, Lords and Commons worked out procedures of appeal and impeachment (the legal process of removing an undesirable official from office), acting, therefore, as the high court of Parliament. The Good Parliament of 1376 elected the first Speaker, Peter de la Mare, to represent the Commons with king and Lords and to establish impeachment procedures.

The next parliament was packed by the opposing faction of John of Gaunt. Richard II was obsessed by his prerogative powers, believing that parliamentary criticism and interference infringed these God-given powers. When, moreover, he questioned his judges on his rights in law they came back with a full defence of the royal prerogatives, which in fact challenged the authority of parliament to have redress of grievances before taxation, and declared that their impeachments were unlawful without royal assent. They added that the king's councillors were his own choice and not responsible to parliament.[5]

A major political crisis ensued in the Merciless Parliament of 1388, culminating in the deposition of Richard II for 'tyranny' and by the establishment of the Lancastrian dynasty by usurpation, although Henry IV claimed the throne of England by right of conquest, hereditary right and recognition by parliament. But the hereditary right was the more significant to the nobility as that determined the right to the possession of lands and titles. Moreover great nobles like Gloucester in 1387, Henry Bolingbroke (Henry IV) in 1399 and the Percy family at the beginning of the fifteenth century revived the ancient tradition that they had a right to take up arms as the natural defenders of the liberties of subjects. The development of links between the crown and the wider political community sought to undermine this traditional role of the higher magnates, but it also gave some of them more incentive to rebel. Most did not; instead they developed their access to royal patronage for offices and rewards as the incomes from their lands fell in the late-fourteenth and early-fifteenth centuries. In turn, the nobility needed to reward their own clients. But then, as a result, the Commons became increasingly suspicious of royal patronage and the oppressive greed of factions of courtiers; they regarded it as monstrous that parliamentary subsidies raised from the lower orders could be used to reward the higher nobility. Major rebellions like the Peasants' Revolt of 1381 and that of Jack Cade in 1450 demonstrated how artisans and peasants could combine politically under leadership of the gentry to demand reforms in the government of the realm.

Parliament as an institution had a slow and troubled history, whereby the Commons began as petitioners and ended as a tax-voting and law-making assembly, as well as performing judicial functions as a high court. However, any interpretation that supports the view of the Whig historians, who saw an inevitable progression from Magna Carta to the ascendancy of the House of Commons in the twentieth century, needs to be avoided.

Henry VIII announced in the sixteenth century:

> We be informed by our judges that we at no time stand so high in our estate royal as in the time of parliament, when we as head and you as members are conjoined and knit together in one body politic.[6]

B. Wilkinson claims that such a pronouncement could have been made at any time in the fifteenth century but especially after 1461. And, finally, on the definition of the very nature of parliament, J. G. Edwards would write:

> the competence of the king in council in parliament was not a 'judicial' competence. It was an omnicompetence. Parliament was a 'high' court, not merely because it was judicially above other courts, but also because it was in itself more than a judicial court; it was an ominicompetent organ of government at the summit of lay affairs in England . . . Parliament's robe of omnicompetence was not a thing of shreds and patches; it was a seamless whole.[7]

When studying the monarchy in this period, we are confronted with a host of questions. What, in effect, is the nature of kingship; what is its role in governing the realm; by what authority do kings rule and what should be the relationship between the ruler and the ruled? Few students of the monarchy would agree today that a royal blood strain has been maintained undefiled since William the Conqueror, thereby making hereditary right the chief justification for kingship. Few, too, would agree that the monarchy as an institution of government evolved in a linear progression from a primitive ability to lead out and fight with conquering hosts of armed forces to a limited, constitutional, parliamentary monarchy such as we have in Britain. However, the longevity of the institution, and its pageantry and symbolism – products of the creative Middle Ages – together with the fluctuations in the political and personal fortunes of royal families cannot fail to fascinate.

Document case study

The monarchy

1.1 The monarch and the law

Sir John Fortescue (1395?–1477?), a noted legal writer, comments on the powers of the monarch

For the king of England is not able to change the laws of his kingdom at pleasure, for he rules his people with a government not only royal but also political. If he were to rule over them with a power only royal, he would be able to change the laws of the realm, and also to impose on them tallages [taxes] and other burdens without consulting them;

this is the sort of dominion which the civil laws indicate when they state that 'What pleased the prince has the force of law.' But it is far otherwise with the king ruling his people politically, because he himself is not able to change the laws without the assent of his subjects nor to burden an unwilling people with strange impositions . . . St Thomas [Aquinas], in the book he wrote for the king of Cyprus, *On Princely Government*, is considered to have desired that a kingdom be constituted in such a way that the king may not be free to govern his people tyrannically, which only comes to pass when the royal power is restrained by political law.

Source: Sir John Fortescue, *On the laws and governance of England*, ed. and tr. by S. Lockwood, Cambridge, 1997, pp. 17–18

1.2 The consecration of the sovereign by anointing with oil

A description of part of the coronation ceremonies

This is the oil with which the kings of England must be anointed but not those wicked ones who now reign or will reign who, on account of their crimes, have lost and will lose much. But kings of the English will arise who will be anointed with this oil and will be good champions of the church. They will recover the lands lost by their forefathers as long as they have the eagle[8] and the phial. Now there will be a king who will be the first to be anointed with this oil; he will recover by force . . . Normandy and Acquitaine . . . as often as he carries this eagle on his breast he shall have victory over all his enemies and his kingdom shall be ever increased.

Source: L. G. W. Legg, *English coronation records*, London, 1901, pp. 169 ff.

1.3 The crown as the supreme symbol of kingship

Shakespeare, in his play Richard II, *makes the king reflect on the fading of the monarch's kingly power*

For God's sake, let us sit upon the ground
And tell sad stories of the death of kings;
How some have been deposed, some slain in war,
Some haunted by the ghosts they have deposed,
Some poisoned by their wives, some sleeping killed,
All murdered. For within the hollow crown
That rounds the mortal temples of a king
Keeps Death his court; and there the antic sits,
Scoffing his state and grinning at his pomp,
Allowing him a breath, a little scene
To monarchise, be feared, and kill with looks,
Infusing him with self and vain conceit,
As if this flesh which walls about our life
Were brass impregnable; and humoured thus,
Comes at the last, and with a little pin
Bores through his castle wall; and farewell, king.

Source: William Shakespeare, *Richard II*, Act III, Scene ii

1.4 Concessions in royal power

Historians of parliament have demonstrated how 'the community of the realm' represented in the Commons gained concessions from the king

Under Edward III (1312–1377) the commons came to act with increasing effect on behalf of the community. The power they gained as a result of their right to grant taxes meant that they won many successes. They compelled, for example, the establishment of gentry keepers, and eventually justices of the peace. They extracted important concessions from the king over such matters as military service and purveyance; their petitions inspired a wide range of legislation. Their interests came gradually to coincide more with those of the magnates, over such questions as labour legislation.

Source: Michael Prestwich, *Parliament and community in fourteenth-century England*, Historical studies, 14, Belfast, 1983, p. 20

1.5 Advice given to the Commons

Sir Nicholas Bacon (1509–1579) Lord Keeper of the Great Seal, advising the House of Commons in 1563 and in 1571

I would advise you to make your laws as plain and as few as may be, for many be burdensome and doubtful to understand. And, secondly, to make them as brief as the matter will suffer [allow]. And, thirdly, that you proceed to the great and weighty matters first, and th'other of smaller importance after. [1563]

[There is need to examine] the want and superfluity of laws . . . whether there be too many laws for anything, which breedeth so many doubts that the subject is sometime to seek how to observe them, and the counsellor how to give advice concerning them. [1571]

Source: T. Hartley, *Proceedings in the parliaments of Elizabeth I*, vol. 1, Leicester, 1993, pp. 78–79, and 183

1.6 The theory of mixed government

A modern historian explains the theory of mixed government which, by the middle of the seventeenth century, had been developed by English political theorists

The English theory of mixed government combined two distinct ideas, and superimposed both on the tangible institutions of King, Lords and Commons. The first was the classical Renaissance idea of mixed government. According to it, there were three pure forms of government; the rule of one, the rule of a few, the rule of many.

Conventionally, though not always, these forms were called monarchy, aristocracy, and democracy. These pure forms were inherently unstable, the vices of one form naturally suggesting the virtues of the next in an endless cycle. Stability, however, could be achieved by mixing the three forms into one government.

Source: M. J. Mendle, 'Politics and political thought: the Body Politic: habits of thought', in C. Russell (ed.), *The origins of the Civil War*, London, 1973, p. 222

Document case-study questions

1 What does Sir John Fortescue mean by 'with a government not only royal but also political' in 1.1?

2 How far does Fortescue view this as a means of restraining the powers of the monarchy?

3 From where, according to 1.2, does the power of the kings of England come? In what respects does this view contrast with that of Fortescue in 1.1?

4 What dimension of kingship does 1.3 add to those shown in 1.1 and 1.2?

5 According to 1.4, what concessions had been given by the monarch to the Commons? What is meant by 'the community of the realm' in this document?

6 What, according to 1.5, was one of the main functions of parliament in the fifteenth century?

7 To what extent would you say that all these documents show that evolution was taking place towards the 'mixed government' described in 1.6?

8 By the fifteenth century, English kingship was regarded as divine, political and imperial. How far do these sources support this assertion?

Notes and references

1 The label 'absolute power' is used in this period as shorthand for the ideology of monarchy, since all monarchies were absolute by definition. There was, however, an emphasis on the God-given nature of supreme royal authority, and a recognition that the king had to rule in accord with divine and natural justice. In this way, historians can make a distinction between absolute monarchy and tyranny. England was a monarchy, therefore it depended for its healthy functioning on the exercise of kingship.

2 *Richard II*, Act III, Scene ii.

3 The career of George Neville (1433?–76) illustrates the vicissitudes of the office of Lord Chancellor, from his appointment in July 1460 until his disgrace, fall and death in June 1476. (See the *Dictionary of national biography*.)

4 The Treasurer, like the Chancellor, also depended on the king's council for his importance (see, for example, the career of John Tiptoft, earl of Worcester 1427–70). (See the *Dictionary of national biography*.)

5 Modern biographers of Richard II, such as Nigel Saul, play down the absolutist image of the king created by Shakespeare's play.

6 B. Wilkinson, *The later Middle Ages in England*, London, 1969, p. 383.

7 Cited in E. Miller, *The origins of parliament*, Historical Association, London, 1960, p. 23.

8 The eagle, the traditional emblem of Roman imperial power was used by the English monarchs as one of the many symbols of royal power. It was not, however, borne on their heraldic shields or on the royal coats of arms.

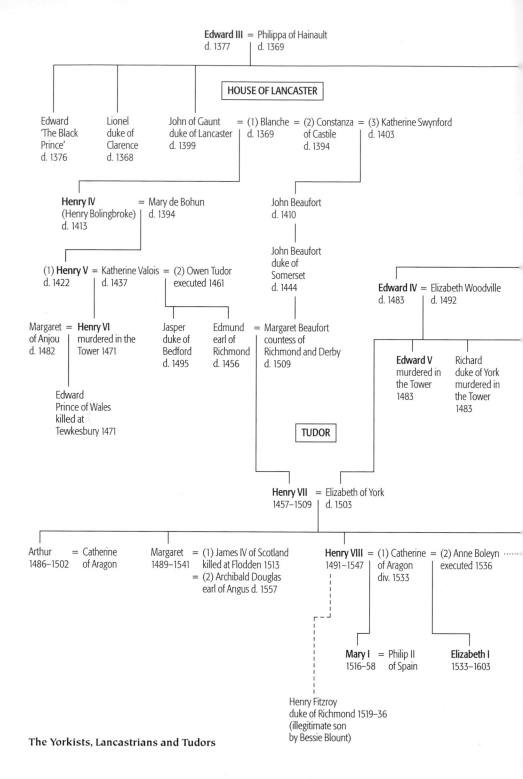

Edward III = Philippa of Hainault
d. 1377 | d. 1369

HOUSE OF LANCASTER

Edward 'The Black Prince' d. 1376

Lionel duke of Clarence d. 1368

John of Gaunt duke of Lancaster d. 1399 = (1) Blanche d. 1369 = (2) Constanza of Castile d. 1394 = (3) Katherine Swynford d. 1403

Henry IV (Henry Bolingbroke) d. 1413 = Mary de Bohun d. 1394

John Beaufort d. 1410

John Beaufort duke of Somerset d. 1444

Edward IV = Elizabeth Woodville
d. 1483 | d. 1492

(1) **Henry V** = Katherine Valois = (2) Owen Tudor
d. 1422 | d. 1437 | executed 1461

Margaret of Anjou d. 1482 = **Henry VI** murdered in the Tower 1471

Jasper duke of Bedford d. 1495

Edmund earl of Richmond d. 1456 = Margaret Beaufort countess of Richmond and Derby d. 1509

Edward V murdered in the Tower 1483

Richard duke of York murdered in the Tower 1483

Edward Prince of Wales killed at Tewkesbury 1471

TUDOR

Henry VII = Elizabeth of York
1457–1509 | d. 1503

Arthur 1486–1502 = Catherine of Aragon

Margaret 1489–1541 = (1) James IV of Scotland killed at Flodden 1513
= (2) Archibald Douglas earl of Angus d. 1557

Henry VIII = (1) Catherine of Aragon div. 1533 = (2) Anne Boleyn executed 1536
1491–1547

Mary I = Philip II of Spain
1516–58

Elizabeth I
1533–1603

Henry Fitzroy duke of Richmond 1519–36 (illegitimate son by Bessie Blount)

The Yorkists, Lancastrians and Tudors

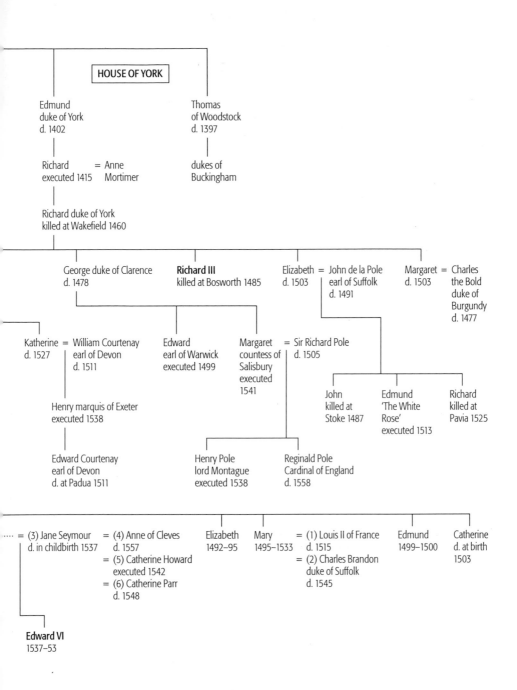

HOUSE OF YORK

Edmund
duke of York
d. 1402

Thomas
of Woodstock
d. 1397

Richard   = Anne
executed 1415   Mortimer

dukes of
Buckingham

Richard duke of York
killed at Wakefield 1460

George duke of Clarence
d. 1478

Richard III
killed at Bosworth 1485

Elizabeth = John de la Pole
d. 1503   earl of Suffolk
             d. 1491

Margaret = Charles
d. 1503   the Bold
           duke of
           Burgundy
           d. 1477

Katherine = William Courtenay
d. 1527   earl of Devon
            d. 1511

Edward
earl of Warwick
executed 1499

Margaret   = Sir Richard Pole
countess of | d. 1505
Salisbury
executed
1541

John
killed at
Stoke 1487

Edmund
'The White
Rose'
executed 1513

Richard
killed at
Pavia 1525

Henry marquis of Exeter
executed 1538

Edward Courtenay
earl of Devon
d. at Padua 1511

Henry Pole
lord Montague
executed 1538

Reginald Pole
Cardinal of England
d. 1558

···· = (3) Jane Seymour
       d. in childbirth 1537

= (4) Anne of Cleves
   d. 1557
= (5) Catherine Howard
   executed 1542
= (6) Catherine Parr
   d. 1548

Elizabeth
1492–95

Mary
1495–1533

= (1) Louis II of France
   d. 1515
= (2) Charles Brandon
   duke of Suffolk
   d. 1545

Edmund
1499–1500

Catherine
d. at birth
1503

Edward VI
1537–53

2 York and Lancaster: the background to the Tudors

The Wars of the Roses

The so-called 'Wars of the Roses' (a label invented by Sir Walter Scott) were fought between the houses of York and Lancaster and began with the Battle of St Albans, on 22 May 1455. Traditionally, they are said to have ended with the Battle of Bosworth Field, on 22 August 1485, although Yorkist opposition was not finally crushed until the Battle of Stoke, on 16 June 1487.

Both houses or aristocratic factions rose to prominence and real power in the long, ineffectual and saintly reign of the Lancastrian king, Henry VI (1422–61; 1470–71). His only son, Edward, was murdered by the Yorkists after the Battle of Tewkesbury in 1471 and, soon after, his widow married the future Richard III. Tradition has it that the red rose became the badge of Edmund, earl of Lancaster in the reign of Edward I and the white rose was one of the identifying badges of the Black Prince, son of Edward III . How the respective colour badges became the distinguishing symbols of York and Lancaster in the fifteenth century is a matter of conjecture.

Militant turbulence amongst the aristocracy characterised the late Middle Ages, as warring factions reduced the power, influence and the wealth of a weak monarchy. The ideals of chivalry, and codes of feudal loyalty and courtly love had long lost their vitality by the fifteenth century, even though monarchs like Edward IV and Henry VII could still pay lip service to the celebrated crusading ideal of medieval Christian Europe. But the main feature of the era is the way in which the feudal aristocracy began to take over control of the machinery of royal government. In this world, which was slowly changing from medieval ideals (still held in theory) to 'the rule of might is right', the gaps between theory and practice, between rich and poor, between corporateness and individualism and between the ambitions and the realities of the emergent national states grew wider. When the Yorkists and early Tudors, therefore, came to revitalise the strength of the crown as the chief governing instrument, their scope could be sometimes enhanced and sometimes restricted by the instrument of parliament. This was in a position to control legislation, taxation, and many areas of local government through the sheriffs, justices of the peace, and down to the meanest constables of the hundreds. However, the principle of rule under the law, by the consent of the natural rulers of the realm (the nobility), and for the good of the commonweal, persisted in England.

The Yorkist ascendancy

The rise of an effective opposition to Henry VI was led by the powerful Richard, duke of York. This opposition had been greatly strengthened by an alliance between York and the influential Neville family after 1454; parliament, too, was pro-Yorkist. Even so, in London and Kent, Richard found 'the people came not to him'. He was able however, to stir up rebellions among those sympathetic to his cause in many towns in three well defined areas: the Welsh Marches, Somerset and Devonshire and East Anglia. His attempted coup by his march on London was foiled by a superior royal force encamped at Blackheath. He was taken prisoner and compelled to seek the king's favour. York was lucky in that Edmund Beaufort, duke of Somerset, whose faction controlled Henry VI, thought it unwise to make a martyr of him at that stage.

In October 1453, Queen Margaret gave birth to a son. This meant that York was no longer Henry's heir, but the ensuing insanity of the king meant that York became Protector in March 1454. The office brought him many allies and a chance to recover his political stature. The queen, however, dominated the king and the court, yet greatly resented not being made regent during her husband's illness. Henry's first illness was short-lived; he had recovered by Christmas 1454. York went north to join the Nevilles and on 22 May 1455 the first battle of the Wars of the Roses took place. The Yorkists had taken the decisive step of opposing the royal standard in arms. Though victorious at St Albans, they prepared a settlement, with the king summoning a parliament in his name, with a Yorkist Speaker and a pro-Yorkist Commons. In the royal household, they sought to replace the predominance of Queen Margaret with their own men.

As a result of the individual victories and defeats of the war and the manoeuvrings of the opposing factions for dominance, England became deeply divided. Because the government ceased to exercise political authority, both parties, by 1459, were ready for civil war. By October 1460, York claimed the throne, but just after Christmas he was defeated and killed at the Battle of Wakefield and his head publicly displayed on the walls of York. The Yorkist cause appeared doomed as Margaret's forces marched south and routed Richard Neville, earl of Warwick, in the second Battle of St Albans. This was a brief conflict but noted in history for the first use of small fire-arms. The king did not want Margaret to march on London, fearing her Welsh and Cheshire levies would run amok in the capital. Meanwhile York's eldest son, Edward, had gathered support from the Welsh Marches and advanced on London. The people, angered by the plunderings of the queen's armies, and the spate of executions after Wakefield and the second Battle of St Albans, gave even more support to the Yorkists under Edward. This popular support enabled Edward to chase the queen's forces north, but also to do this as the accepted king of the realm for, on 4 March 1461, Edward seated himself on a throne in Westminster Hall and was hailed by people and supporters as the rightful hereditary king. On Palm Sunday, 29 March, Edward's forces overtook the Lancastrians in a snowstorm at Towton, in Yorkshire. With the help of John Mowbray, duke of Norfolk, they inflicted a frightful slaughter on the queen's forces. Henry VI, Margaret and their son Edward fled to Scotland. The stubborn courage of Margaret kept up a rearguard action against Edward IV, by joining a Lancastrian rising in the North in 1464. It failed as the Scots' support dwindled and Henry VI, virtually on the run in the Lake District, was finally captured at Clitheroe, sent to Edward and thence to the Tower.

The credit for the Yorkist campaign in the North went to Richard Neville, earl of Warwick, whose vast connections formed the core of the Yorkist party. His popularity as a military leader and as a liberal aristocrat, together with his courage and energy, made Warwick the most distinguished and powerful man in all England in the early days of Edward's reign. By contrast, the new Yorkist king seemed to be a dissolute youth who, when not fighting, cared only for wine, women and pageantry. This superficial, pleasure loving exterior won him much popularity, but it disguised real political ability and the ruthlessness of the Renaissance despot which he truly was.

The house of York was to occupy the throne for less than twenty years, but the price of that achievement was 31 peers killed and 20 executed. The English nobility was embroiled in a blood feud, but few families were utterly wiped out in the wars. The treason trials, vendettas, assassinations and attainders had, in effect, become the weapons of party politics, and the results of this would long outlive the Yorkists as family feuds and national politics became mixed.

Edward IV

Shakespeare's 'Now is the winter of our discontent Made glorious summer by this sun of York' echoed the popularity of the young, militarily victorious Edward; would he give the nation a period of peace and prosperity? But Edward was never allowed to forget that he owed his throne to his cousin Richard Neville, earl of Warwick and Salisbury, who was equally popular as a courageous military figure especially in the war against France. Repeated Lancastrian risings disturbed what should have been a confident and efficient reign. Edward who had gained the crown by force of arms in 1461, would then lose it between 1469 and 1471 by the treachery of his former ally Warwick. The earl had been alienated by Edward's marriage to Elizabeth Woodville, the widow and daughter of Lancastrians, and whose two sons, five brothers and seven sisters built up a formidable clique at court in opposition to Warwick and the Nevilles. For a time, Edward was forced into exile by Warwick and George, duke of Clarence, the king's own brother, until returning to England in March 1471 and landing in the Humber, he organised enough support to march on London and regain his throne.

Three years after the incarceration and death of Henry VI in 1471, the final Lancastrian stronghold, Harlech Castle, capitulated; the Yorkist Edward IV had triumphed.

The restoration of government

The year 1471 saw the end of Lancastrian hopes and the end of Edward's perils; indeed, the year marked the end of a long era of weakness in the institution of monarchy and the beginning of over a century of strength.

To counteract the widespread instability in the government, Edward did much to build up a secure crown and efficient and effective government and, above all, he meant to 'live of his own', that is to use the royal revenue of about £28,000 a year for all the calls on his income and patronage. Customs brought in about £34,000 a year, tithes were collected with greater insistence, and the king's personal estates were better administered. All of this helped to keep down taxation, which was a sure way to gain the hearts of Englishmen. But did such political expediency in letting sleeping dogs lie in the matter of taxation leave the monarchy weaker, in the long run, in the face of later parliaments? Government was still highly personal: a king had to be able to control his magnates and gain their respect and support for his policies and, in this, the personal bond of loyalty was still vital to good government.

The ranks of the nobility had been thinned by battle and execution, the crown's endemic poverty had been remedied by the acquisition of the huge estates of the house of York, as well as by confiscations of lands for treason, although much had been restored to those pardoned. We should not, moreover, exaggerate, as contemporaries may have done, the devastation of the so-called Wars of the Roses, for in the total period from 1455 to 1487 there was hardly thirteen weeks of actual hostilities. This is because the campaigns were brief and fought out between the soldiery of the nobility and barely impinged on the daily routine of the ordinary bulk of the population. However, historians still differ as to whether the memories of the brutalities, disorder and impoverishment of the wars made the English populace more ready to submit to future arbitrary and oppressive government than to resort to rebellion. Perhaps the most important result of the wars was the change in the role of the nobility; never again did they form a united front against the king; their quarrels were purely factional with no constitutional ideals to give them a moral ascendancy.

When Edward died, England was quiet and in a degree of order and, although he left the monarchy wealthy, it was not politically strong because his son, the would-be Edward V, was a minor. Edward IV began his reign at the age of nineteen, and in debt, and when he died in 1483 at the age of forty – possibly from acute appendicitis – he was the first English king for centuries to die with cash in the treasury.

Richard III

Edward's successor was his son, Edward, a boy of twelve. The newly found strength of the monarchy could be ruined in feuds between the boy's maternal relatives, the Woodvilles and Greys and his paternal uncle, Richard duke of Gloucester. Richard had married Anne, daughter of Warwick, the dead 'King Maker' and co-heiress of the vast Warwick estates. Fear of civil strife may help to account for the easy usurpation of Richard as king, but he was also a proven soldier, leader and administrator. Tudor propaganda would later brand Richard as a monster who had killed Henry VI and his son, and also his own brother, Clarence, in 1478. Apparently, in 1483, there were no such suspicions and he gained popular support because he struck out at the unpopular Woodvilles and Greys. But Richard, in removing all opposition to his accession, had the young Edward V and his brother shut up in the Tower. He went on to have his brother's marriage declared illegal and consequently to have the princes and their sisters declared bastards so that he then became the sole legitimate heir to the throne. He may well have had his nephews murdered in the Tower. (See J. Gillingham (ed.) in Select bibliography, p. 112.)

In any event, their deaths made Richard's position precarious as it split the Yorkists and gave the Lancastrians renewed hopes, especially under the able leadership of the duke of Buckingham. He turned from being the king's chief supporter to being his deadly foe in rebellion, and his likely rival for the throne itself. Certainly, he became the centre of a conspiracy throughout the west and south of England against Richard, now regarded as 'the usurper of the realm'. Buckingham seems to have assumed that the sons of Edward IV were either dead or doomed in the Tower. Did he covet the throne himself, as a direct descendant of Edward III and married to a Woodville? He also had met Margaret, countess of Richmond, survivor of the Beaufort line and her son Henry Tudor, earl of Richmond. Therefore Buckingham must have recognised that, even if the Yorkists were utterly set aside, Margaret and her son would stand between him and the throne.

Margaret asked him to obtain the king's permission to have her son Henry married to Elizabeth of York, one of Edward IV's daughters. Richard was unlikely to agree, as such an alliance would have been contrary to all his interests, but Buckingham saw in it the union of the claims of both York and Lancaster and, as such, the basis for a firm alliance against Richard. He planned a massive rebellion, with simultaneous risings in Wales, Wiltshire, Devonshire, Kent and Sussex and, with the aid of forces recruited by Henry Tudor, earl of Richmond, from the duke of Brittany, a landing in Wales. But all went wrong, as foul weather dispersed the forces from Brittany, and storms flooded the Severn basin, preventing Buckingham from meeting up with forces from Devon. Richard's men put down the risings with vigour; support for Buckingham melted away as the usual spate of executions ensued. Richard lost no time in having Buckingham himself captured and executed.

Order was restored throughout the realm and Richard strove for popularity by acts of parliament to put an end to the Benevolences which Edward IV had extorted, to suppress intimidation and acts of corruption in the law courts, and to encourage internal and external trade. Even so, Richard had to face increasing and formidable hostility, despite his courage, generosity and general efficiency in government. To add to his problems, his only son, the Prince of Wales, died in April 1484, and Anne, his wife, could bear no further children. To strengthen the defences of the realm against invasion from the obvious rival claimant and successor to his throne, the Lancastrian Henry Tudor, Richard had recourse to unpopular Forced Loans which inevitably weakened the already narrow basis of his power.

When Henry landed at Milford Haven in August 1485, he was able to recruit heavily in his native Wales. His grandfather, Owen Tudor, executed by the

Yorkists in 1461, had married (if indeed he had married) Henry V's widow, Catherine of France, and their son, Edmund, had married the Lady Margaret Beaufort. Henry Tudor, therefore, could trace his descent through his mother from Edward III and on his father's side he could at least claim French royal blood. Propagandists would later claim that he could trace his descent from Cadwallader and the ancient kings of Britain right back to King Arthur, but this is still a matter of historical conjecture. Henry's main strength lay in the mounting hostility to Richard, and he also finely calculated the amount of treachery there would be among Richard's followers when it came to a battle.

Henry's march into the Midlands to meet Richard in battle in Leicestershire at Bosworth is well known. Though Richard had the larger army, the desertions from his standard, including the immensely influential Stanleys and Percys, cost him the victory. Richard died fighting Henry's central forces. Apparently the crown was found on the field of battle and placed on Henry's head by Lord Stanley. Richard's naked body was exposed to the public in Leicester and later buried at Grey Friars. The alabaster tomb erected by Henry VII was plundered at the dissolution of the monasteries in Henry VIII's reign and Richard's body thrown into the River Soar. Bosworth Field is often considered to be highly significant as it heralded the foundation of a new dynasty but did it also mark (as many have claimed) the end of medieval England?

Document case study

Edward IV and Richard III

2.1 The violence of fifteenth-century aristocracy

From the Paston letters, *written between 1422 and 1509*

In this country every man is well willing to go with my lords here; and I hope God shall help them, for the people in the North rob and steal and be appointed to pill [plunder] all this country and give away men's goods and livelihoods in all the south country, and that will ask a mischief. My lords that be here have as much as they may do to keep down all this country, more than four or five shires; for they would be upon the men in the North for it is for the weal of all the South.

Source: J. Gairdner (ed.), *The Paston letters*, vol. 3, London, 1904, p. 250

2.2 Civil war

A contemporary historian, Polydore Vergil, describes the condition of England in the mid-fifteenth century

This, finally was the end of foreign war, and likewise the renewing of civil calamity; for when the fear of outward enemy, which as yet kept the kingdom in good exercise, was gone from the nobility, such was the contention among them for glory and sovereignty, that even then the people were apparently divided into two factions, according as it fell out afterwards, when those two, that is to say, king Henry, who derived his pedigree from the House of Lancaster and Richard duke of York, who conceived himself by his mother's side from Lionel, son to Edward the Third contended mutually for the kingdom. By means whereof their two factions grew shortly so great through the whole realm . . . that many men were utterly destroyed, and the whole realm brought to ruine and decay.

Source: Polydore Vergil, *Anglica historia*, Books 23–25 (1422–85), ed. and tr. by H. Ellis, Camden Society, vol. 29, London, 1844, pp. 93–94

2.3 A pen portrait of Edward IV

Sir Thomas More writing in his unfinished Life of Richard III, *c. 1513*

He was a goodly personage and very princely to behold, of heart courageous, politic in counsel, in adversity nothing abashed, in prosperity rather joyful than proud, in peace just and merciful, in war sharp and fierce, in the field bold and hardy . . . He was of visage lovely, of body mighty, strong and clean made. Howbeit in latter days, with over liberal diet, somewhat corpulent and burly, and nevertheless not uncomely, he was of youth greatly given to fleshly wantonness.

Source: R. S. Sylvester (ed.), *The complete works of St Thomas More*, vol. 2.4, New Haven, 1965–76, p. 4

2.4 How the news of Edward's death spread in London

Sir Thomas More writing in his Life of Richard III, *1513*

The self night in which King Edward IV died, one Mystlebrooke, long ere morning, came in great haste to the house of one Potter, dwelling in Red Cross Street without Cripplegate. And when he was with hasty rapping quickly letten in, he showed unto Potter that King Edward was departed. 'By my throth man,' quoth Potter, 'then will my master the Duke of Gloucester be king.'

Source: R. S. Sylvester (ed.), *The complete works of St Thomas More*, vol. 2.4, New Haven, 1965–76, p. 4

2.5 The courage of Richard III

From the Croyland *(Crowland)* chronicle *in Lincolnshire. Before 1483, Richard III spent most of his life in northern England, and northern sources draw a more favourable picture of him than do the sources from the south of England. But there is general agreement about his courage, even from hostile writers*

There now began a very fierce battle between the two sides; Henry, earl of Richmond with his knights advanced directly upon King Richard . . . in the end a glorious victory was granted by heaven to the earl of Richmond, now sole king, together with the priceless crown which King Richard had previously worn. As for King Richard he received many mortal wounds, and like a spirited and most courageous prince, fell in battle on the field and not in flight.

Source: *The Croyland chronicle*, A. R. Myers (ed.), *English historical documents, 1327–1485*, vol. 4, London, 1969

2.6 The loyalty of the city of York to Richard III

The view of the city councillors after the death of the king (Minute of the York city council, 23 August 1485)

Minute: The throne being vacant . . . King Richard late mercifully reigning upon us was through great treason . . . piteously slain and murdered to the great heaviness of this city.

York city council archives, see R. J. Green, *York city archives*, York, 1971

2.7 Two views of the character of Richard III

William Camden, the Elizabethan court historian, assesses the character of Richard III

Richard by all persons of reflection is esteemed a bad man but a good king.

Source: William Camden, *Britannia*, vol. 1, ed. by R. Gough, London, 1806, p. 386

A modern historian on Richard III

Yet even in Tudor days men sometimes dared to speak good of him, and not only in the north of England. In 1525 Cardinal Wolsey was pressing the mayor and aldermen of London for a benevolence. To their objection that this demand was contrary to a statute of Richard III the cardinal retorted: 'I marvell that you speak of Richard III who was a usurper and a murderer of his own nephews.' The reply to this retort . . . might serve as a partial epitaph on Richard III: 'although he did evill, yet in his tyme wer many good actes made.'

A. R. Myers, 'The character of Richard III', *History today*, vol. 4 no. 8, 1954, p. 521

Document case-study questions

1 What impression can be gained from all the documents about the violence of the mid-fifteenth century? Why was the aristocracy a threat to law and order?

2 What type of person do you think Edward IV was? Use the documents to support your conclusion.

3 Sir Thomas More was five years old when Edward IV died. How does this affect the reliability of his character study?

4 William Camden suggests that Richard III was 'a bad man but a good king'. How far do the documents on Richard III support this view?

5 Why has Richard III had such a bad press? To what extent was he liked in the north of England?

6 Shakespeare's play, *Richard III*, portrays the king as a bloodthirsty murderer. To what extent was Shakespeare in this context a publicity agent for the Tudor dynasty?

3 Henry VII: 1485–1509

An early Tudor portrait of King Henry VII in middle age (English School, sixteenth century). Did the beginning of his reign mark the end of medieval England or could Henry VII claim to be the most efficient of late medieval monarchs?

The foundation of the Tudor dynasty

The Battle of Bosworth has traditionally been thought of as a landmark that divides the medieval from the modern in English history. But, as far as central and local government, and the economic and social aspects of life were concerned, the reign of the first Tudor, Henry VII, was little different from that of his immediate predecessors. He inherited all the institutions of government, together with their personnel, that had operated under Edward IV. Henry's aims and methods were also those of Edward and, because they had similar problems, Henry adopted similar policies. Henry's use of the council through a body of close advisers and frequent meetings made the council the effective centre of government and administration. His problems, as those of the Yorkists had been, were centred around his claim to the throne, and the inevitable challenges to this; his efforts to consolidate royal power; his promotion of a harder-working nobility and gentry; the struggle to build up royal finances (which necessarily entailed the use of parliament); and the avoidance of costly wars abroad. Like his predecessors, his relations with Scotland, Ireland and Wales were inextricably mixed up with the attempts to secure and consolidate his own power and the future of the Tudor dynasty. In these respects, and especially in his business-like qualities, Henry could be considered the most efficient of the late medieval monarchs.

Henry VII: his character and abilities

Henry Tudor was the son of Edmund Tudor, earl of Richmond, and Margaret Beaufort, the heiress of John of Gaunt. He was brought up in Wales by his uncle, Jasper Tudor. His mother, Margaret, was widowed at the age of thirteen, three months before the birth of Henry, her only child, at Pembroke Castle on 27 January 1457. Henry became head of the house of Lancaster in 1471 on the death (or murder) of Henry VI, but during Edward IV's reign he became a refugee in Brittany. Apart from his innate ability and good fortune, Henry owed much of his success in securing the throne to the determination and political sense of his mother Margaret. She helped to arrange his marriage to Elizabeth of York, kept him well supplied with money and, in effect, helped to organise the 1483 rebellion. Strictly speaking, she was the true Lancastrian heir, but she took little part in politics once her son was securely on the throne.

Polydore Vergil, the court historian, who knew Henry well, described his appearance towards the end of his life – he was only fifty-two when he died:

> His body was slender but well built and strong; his height above the average. His appearance was remarkably attractive and his face was cheerful especially when speaking; his eyes were small and blue; his teeth few, poor and blackish; his hair was thin and grey; his complexion pale.

Francis Bacon tells us that his countenance was 'reverend, and a little like a churchman' and that the only two women in his life were his mother 'whom he reverenced much' and that 'towards his queen he was nothing uxorious, nor scarce indulgent; but companionable and respective, and without jealousy'. Unlike her mother, Elizabeth Woodville, the queen did not indulge in political intrigue.

Henry's administration: law and order and finance

Contemporaries agree that Henry VII loved justice, repressed violence, ended internal faction and won a reputation in Europe for the wisdom of his statecraft. He enjoyed the business of government and apparently supervised most departments. This was especially true of the nation's accounts, for he initialled many of the financial records himself. It is not clear, however, to what extent his agents, Sir Richard Empson and Edmund Dudley, used extortion on the king's behalf to build up a healthy treasury. Henry may very well have kept the trust and faith of his parliaments by not asking them to grant taxes too often, but he made up for this by fully exploiting all traditional sources of the royal revenue. Dudley became a tireless tax collector and, while so doing, feathered his own nest. Henry VII did not feel secure unless he was rich. A full treasury helps to explain why he was successful in quelling the rebellions against him; and it took him 15 years before he could feel safe from rival claimants.

Abroad, Margaret of Burgundy, sister to Edward IV, encouraged revolts. In 1487 Lambert Simnel announced that he was Edward, earl of Warwick, then in the Tower. He was crowned 'Edward VI' in Dublin because of the overwhelming support for the Yorkists in Ireland, but Henry put down his supporters at the Battle of Stoke in 1487.[1] Perkin Warbeck's claim to be Richard, duke of York, the younger son of Edward IV, supposedly murdered by his uncle Richard III, was more dangerous to Henry VII. This was because he was supported by the Scottish king, James IV, in 1496. Warbeck's landing in Cornwall in 1497 failed; he was captured, but not executed until 1499. This was the last notable attempt to rebel against Henry VII.

Most historians agree that Henry was a genius at organisation. The ways in which he consolidated the monarchy, laying the foundations of Tudor power, clearly demonstrate that ability. His breaking-up of the feudal power of the nobility, often referred to as 'bastard feudalism', was made easier to some degree by the extinction of some noble lines in the wars.[2] The king took over their estates and the lands of those attainted for having fought for Richard III. He forbade the practices of livery and maintenance and, when the local courts proved too weak to enforce fines, Henry set up a council 'Learned in the Law' in 1495 to deal with influential lords. This court, not to be confused with the celebrated Star Chamber Court, was a small body of a dozen members who saw to the collection of all feudal dues and debts owed to the crown and brought defaulters to justice.[3] Because he had a monopoly of gunpowder, Henry could take even more drastic measures, such as levelling keeps and castles if the barons persisted in opposing the monarch. The result was that Henry Tudor was the first English monarch not to be surrounded by barons whose united wealth and power were greater than his own. But this aspect of his rule must not be exaggerated – many nobles still owned great estates and therefore kept political influence.

It is often stated that Henry promoted 'the new middle-class country gentlemen' to counterbalance the power of the nobility; this too, must not be overstated. Henry's council had a mixture of nobles, clerics, lawyers and country gentlemen, many of whom were related to the great families of the land. Indeed, half of Henry's councillors had served Edward IV. While there was a mercantile middle class on the move and on the make – Empson, for example – it was very small and still had to make its way into the corridors of power.

Furthermore, while Henry also used every means at his disposal to increase royal wealth there was nothing new about his financial methods. Like Edward IV, he husbanded the proceeds from royal estates and exacted the full feudal dues from his rights of Wardship, Marriage, Promotions and Death incidents and he levied Forced Loans and Benevolences. He cleverly manipulated trade and foreign policy to his own financial advantage. Finally, he could also manage to get 'extraordinary' supplies from parliament. However, parliament was only called seven times during his reign. In fact, in every department of government Henry simply used the old institutions of council and of parliament more efficiently than his Yorkist predecessors. In that sense he did not create a 'new system of government'; it was rather the amount of crown wealth which he amassed, not its government or institutions, which is the most innovatory aspect of the new Tudor monarchy. He revived former provincial councils which had decayed to control rebellious areas, for example the Council in the Marches of Wales and the Council of the North. Overall the king's council was the centre of administration, the instrument of policy making and the final means for dispensing royal justice, and it was, therefore, the chief arena of political conflict.

Henry VII and Wales

By 1415, Wales had been irreversibly conquered, but the conquest did not bring political or governmental unity. Wales remained a mixture of private lordships and royal shires until well into the sixteenth century. In R. R. Davies's words, 'It was treated, in effect, as a collection of colonial annexes dependent on the crown and higher aristocracy of England.'[4] And yet it preserved its linguistic unity and literary traditions and a continued self-awareness among its peoples. The Council in the Marches of Wales was a development from the Council of the Prince of Wales. This had been set up to administer the prince's estates in Wales in the reign of Edward IV but it later lapsed. Henry VII made it a permanent institution for his son Prince Arthur and, after Arthur's death in 1502, it continued as the Council in the Marches of Wales. It was not given statutory powers until the Act of Union with Wales in 1536 and then had power to appoint sheriffs and justices of the peace. Through it, the semi-independent Marcher lords had to acknowledge the authority of the English crown. In time, the Tudor policy in Wales would see a fairly successful replacement of traditional Welsh landholding systems based on kinship and gavelkind[5] with an English-style squirearchy of freeholders.

The Council of the North

Edward IV and Richard III had appointed a Council of the North of England where the great border families of Percy, Neville, Scrope and Dacre ruled like independent princes with their own forces and with aristocratic authority. But Henry VII gradually made the intermittent Council of the North a virtual offshoot of his own council. He had to defend the country against the vigilant foe to the north and, like the Lancastrians and Yorkists before him, he had to entrust the defence of the frontier to the men of the frontier. He thus faced the dilemma of what to do should frontiersmen turn their arms against the government. Henry soon realised that to govern the north of England he needed a Percy, hence he had to release the great earl of Northumberland from the Tower and restore him as Lord Warden of the East and Middle Marches.[6] If possible, the council was to meet at York once a quarter to 'order and examine' all bills of complaint; it had powers to deal with 'riots, forcible entries, distress takings (robberies) and all other misbehaviours, against our laws and peace' and offenders were to be lodged in one of the royal castles. Finally, all orders coming from the council were to be headed 'By the king' and endorsed at the end 'And by his council'. It seems that Henry's mother, the countess of Richmond, and her circle had a strong influence on the North and in the Council of the North, and that Empson, his notorious tax-collector, also had some special authority in the North.[7]

Henry's concern for law and order can also be seen in his revival of the justices of the peace in local government; they were mostly landed gentry but their authority had dwindled; the king was determined to reward loyalty and so gain willing servants to restore sound government and economic prosperity. However, some of the 'newer' appointees proved to be as corrupt as the professional lawyer class with whom they came into conflict.[8]

Foreign affairs

Relations abroad were subordinated to the need for the new dynasty to be recognised and respected, a necessity which usurpers had long realised. Traditional hostility to France was still strong in England despite the help given by Charles VIII in financing the expedition that had led to Bosworth. It flared up again over French ambitions to annexe Brittany. Henry announced his intention to assert his claim to the French crown, yet cut short his expensive expedition to France in October 1492 in order to secure a favourable treaty with France at Etaples. In that treaty Charles VIII secured England's neutrality in his wars in Italy but he paid £150,000 to Henry for the privilege. It did not end English claims on France as they were revived in Henry VIII's time.

Henry VII's more famous foreign alliance, however, was the 1489 Treaty of Medina del Campo with Spain. This treaty provided for the marriage of his eldest son, Prince Arthur, with the young Spanish princess, Catherine of Aragon, when they both reached marriageable age, greatly enhancing Henry's prestige abroad.

Catherine's dowry to the prince on their marriage in 1501 was retained when she later married the future Henry VIII. Spain also made commercial concessions and Henry's treasury benefited from the increased trade which followed. Part of the agreement was war with France and, believing Henry's threats to wage war in 1492, Charles VIII made peace, as we have seen, on payment of a huge indemnity. Furthermore, since parliament had already voted money for the war, Henry virtually doubled his money.

By 1496, both France and the Emperor Maximilian courted English support for their Italian wars and, once again, Henry allowed himself to be bought off by the emperor, who agreed to a trade treaty between the ruler of the Netherlands, Philip of Burgundy, and Henry VII. This was the *Magnus Intercursus*, which was highly favourable to England. English merchants would be able to sell their goods wholesale anywhere in the duke of Burgundy's lands (except Flanders) without paying any tolls or customs. Henry went further to promote trade by agreement with other foreign powers such as Florence in 1490 and Denmark in 1496. In 1506, he negotiated yet another commercial treaty with Philip of Burgundy. But, even so, he had to confirm the privileges of the German Hanseatic League merchants in England in 1486 and again in 1504.

Henry hardly realised the future impact that his letters patent in 1496 to John Cabot and his sons would have. These were Genoese merchant adventurers, who had settled in Bristol, and were planning a voyage westwards across the North Atlantic. They were required to return any goods to Bristol, and were granted a monopoly of any trade they developed in the course of their maritime enterprises.

Marriage alliances and trade were both made instruments of policy; Henry's daughter Margaret married King James IV of Scotland – a union which cut across the ancient and dangerous alliance between France and Scotland – the 'Auld Alliance'. This marriage ensured a period of peace between England and her northern neighbour. James IV was strong and well loved in Scotland but he had to rid himself of the baronial factions that had opposed his father. Scottish forays into northern England continued the menace of lawlessness. It was not until the union of the two crowns under James VI and I that border anarchy abated.

Henry VII and Ireland

From 1470 to 1534, three successive earls of Kildare, Old English in origin, that is to say, descendants of the original Anglo-Norman, twelfth-century settlers, virtually ruled those areas of Ireland subject to the English crown. These consisted mainly of the Pale, which, by the sixteenth century, was a territory stretching in a thirty-mile radius from Dublin and certain garrison towns throughout the island. The delegation of royal authority to the earls of Kildare – the Fitzgeralds – meant that the English monarch need not concern himself directly with Ireland. The eighth earl of Kildare, Garret (Gearóid Mór in the Celtic sources) Fitzgerald was pardoned by Henry for his support of the Yorkist pretenders and his restoration as Lord Deputy in 1496 began a period of uninterrupted Kildare rule in Ireland that lasted until 1519. The main reason was financial, as the Kildares were able to govern in the king's name without calls on the English revenue. This was because, after 1496, the major portion of royal revenues in Ireland was paid directly to Kildare for his civil and military administration in the defence of English interests. There is no evidence that the 'great earl', as he was called, wished to sever his links with the English crown and rule Ireland as a separate entity, nor is there any evidence that Henry VII wanted to abandon his reliance on Kildare as his agent of royal authority. The great earl and his son married into the English aristocracy; his second wife was Elizabeth St John, a relative of Henry Tudor – but five of their surviving sons and a nephew, Thomas (Silken Thomas), were to die on the scaffold in 1537. His son, Gearóid Óg, the ninth earl of Kildare, returned to Ireland in 1503, aged sixteen, already married to Elizabeth Zouche, but she died in 1517. Three years later, he married Elizabeth Gray, daughter of the marquis of Dorset. In this way the Fitzgeralds of Kildare were part of the circle of the English nobility.

It is significant that Kildare tried sporadically to extend his authority into the west and south-west at the expense of leading Gaelic Irish families and especially against the other rival old English families like the O'Briens of Thomond, the Burkes of Connaught and the Butlers, earls of Ormonde.[9] The famous 'Kildare Rental' entitled 'Duties upon Irishmen' shows a long list of Gaelic Irish leaders paying tribute to the Kildares and this adoption of practices from within the Gaelic political system was one of the main reasons for the general success of the Kildares.[10]

However, the Old English colony (also known, less appropriately, as Anglo-Irish), resented the extortionate methods of the Kildares and saw their government as acting against the best interests of the Old English colony in Ireland. This is one reason for a spate of reform plans and treatises originating from London and the Pale calling for the revitalisation of English law, custom and practice within Ireland. Indeed, this would have amounted to nothing less than a programme of Anglicisation, with some limited schemes of recolonisation. These reform plans may also be seen as a reaction to Irish support for Perkin Warbeck which, in turn, led to the appointment of Sir Edward Poynings as Governor and the dismissal of Kildare. The celebrated 'Poynings' Law' of 1494 restricted legislation in the Irish parliament. No bill, for example, could be introduced until it had been approved by London. This was all in very marked contrast to the policies pursued by the Kildares in the previous 40 years. These had favoured working within the Gaelic political system rather than trying radically to change it, thereby reinforcing the Gaelic revival of the earlier fifteenth century which had halted Anglicisation.

Kildare was reinstated as Lord Deputy, and in 1508 he was licensed to summon a parliament, the first since 1499. Its sessions resulted in the renewal of a ten-year subsidy;[11] all other bills including the regulation of trade were suspended on the news of Henry VII's death on 21 April 1509.

Henry's achievements

General assessments of Henry VII and his reign tend to emphasise his practical good sense, statesmanship, financial acuity (if not downright extortion) and all the methods he used to put the future Tudors on a sound footing. He has some claim to be regarded as the greatest of his dynasty. He kept the crown seized from the head of a rival slain in battle. He built a strong orderly government out of chaos, but by using existing institutions. He handed on to his son a secure throne, an undisputed succession, a full treasury, established prestige abroad and a prosperous foreign trade. Ironically, while Henry VII carefully avoided basing his claim on his marriage to Edward IV's daughter, his successor, Henry VIII, a son of Elizabeth of York, could claim to be king of England on perfectly legitimist Yorkist principles.

Document case study

Henry VII

3.1 A portrait of the king

From Polydore Vergil's English history, *an important source for the reign of Henry VII*

Henry reigned twenty-three years and seven months. He lived fifty-two years. By his wife Elizabeth he had eight children, four boys and the same number of girls. Three survived him, an only son, Henry prince of Wales and two daughters, Margaret married to James king of Scotland, and Mary betrothed to Charles, prince of Castile . . . He was distinguished, wise, and prudent in character . . . He had a most tenacious memory and was not devoid of scholarship . . . in government he was shrewd . . . none got the better of him by deceit or sharp practice . . . by nature he preferred peace to war. Above all he cherished justice so that he punished with the utmost vigour, robberies, murders, and every other kind of crime . . . in his later days all these virtues were obscured by avarice . . . and in a monarch it is the worst of all vices, since it hurts everyone, and distorts those qualities of trust, justice and integrity with which a kingdom should be governed.

Source: Polydore Vergil, *Anglica historia* (1485–1537), ed. and tr. by D Hay, Camden Series, vol. 74, London, 1950, pp. 142–46

3.2 Henry VII's methods of collecting his royal dues

A Commission from the patent rolls, 7 August, 1486

Commission to John Fisher, serjeant at law, John Mordaunte, Richard Godfrey, Richard Sheldon, John Stanford and William Collet, to enquire in the county of Bedford of all concealed lands, goods and chattels, and of lands given in mortmain without licence [transferred to religious houses or corporations without royal permit]; and of all lands acquired by Edward IV and Richard III and who were enfeoffed of them to the use of those kings . . . and to certify the king hereof in the Exchequer; also of all lands which the persons named in a schedule annexed held at their death in the said county.

Source: *Calendar of patent rolls*, Henry VII, vol. 1, 1485–1494, no. 133, HMSO, London

3.3 The composition of Henry's council

From Polydore Vergil's Anglica historia

He established a Council in his household by whose opinion all things should be justly and rightly governed and causes brought to it to be decided without the bitterness of lawsuits. And for this Council he chose men renowned for their singular shrewdness, loyalty and reliability, John, earl of Oxford; Jasper, duke of Bedford; Thomas Stanley, earl of Derby . . . John Morton, bishop of Ely, Richard Fox, Edward Poynings . . . and he chose other wise men to counsel for specific business among whom were Richard Thomas, a Welshman . . . Thomas Gray, marquis of Dorset, a good and prudent man, George Talbot, earl of Shrewsbury, wise and moderate in all things; Thomas, earl of Ormond, an Irishman, William Say, a prominent knight . . . Thomas Howard, earl of Surrey, a man of the greatest wisdom, reliability and loyalty . . . William Blount, Lord Mountjoy, very well spoken and cultured . . . and many other good counsellors and the chief bishops . . .

Source: Polydore Vergil, *Anglica historia* (1485–1537), ed. and tr. by D. Hay, Camden Series, vol. 74, London, 1950, pp. 5–6

3.4 The power of Henry's son as prince of Wales

A commission from the patent rolls, 20 March 1493

Power during pleasure to Arthur, prince of Wales, duke of Cornwall and earl of Chester and Flint to appoint King's justices of oyer and terminer in the counties of Salop, Hereford, Gloucester and Worcester and the marches of Wales adjoining those counties and in Wales; to array men at arms, archers, and other fencible men [swordsmen] there for defence . . . Power also to him to have retainers by livery or by oaths . . . power also to be the King's Justice to enquire by jury of the marches of Wales of all liberties, privileges and franchises in the possession of any person soever . . . which in future ought to be seized into the King's hands.

Source: *Calendar of patent rolls*, Henry VII, vol. 1, 1485–1494, p. no. 438, HMSO, London

3.5. The nature of Henry VII's financial policy

The historian, G. R. Elton, writing in 1974

Down to about 1495 the king and his ministers were mainly engaged in extending the operation of the royal prerogative and erecting a system which would bring in the maximum return from landed revenues and feudal rights. The system received further elaboration later when the death of its chief agent, Bray, made it advisable to settle specific tasks on selected councillors: in 1503 John Husse was appointed master of wards, and in 1508 Sir Edward Belknap became surveyor of the prerogative. But the main work consisted in the extension of the king's legal claims and this was quite complete by 1495. In the years that followed it appears that Henry turned to the problems of the penal statutes and from 1500 an organisation for their enforcement existed.

Source: G. R. Elton, 'Henry VII: rapacity and remorse', in *Studies in Stuart politics and government*, vol. 1, Cambridge, 1974, pp. 57–58

1 What impression of Henry's character is given by Polydore Vergil in 3.1?

2 What is the purpose of the commission given to the persons mentioned in 3.2?

3 In what respects does 3.1 help to explain why a commission was issued to John Fisher?

4 In what ways, in 3.3, does Polydore Vergil view the council as central to Henry VII's government?

5 How was Henry's council balanced? Why do you think this was important?

6 Explain, using 3.4, the powers that Arthur, prince of Wales had over the Principality and the Marches.

7 Henry VII is often criticised as both rapacious and avaricious. How far do these documents support or refute this argument?

Notes and references

1 Margaret of Burgundy supplied 2,000 German mercenaries but they and the rebels suffered heavily at Stoke (near Newark) on 16 June 1487; that battle marked the end of the Wars of the Roses.

2 See particularly, M. Hicks' work in the Select bibliography on p. 112.

3 Henry was not the originator of the Court of Star Chamber to deal with the 'overmighty subject'. Seventeenth-century commentators misread Tudor documents relating to the Star Chamber Act of 1487 which indeed Henry VII had passed to set up a special court to deal with offences against public order. The Court of Star Chamber itself was a branch of the king's council acting in its judicial capacity.

4 R. R. Davies, *The age of conquest, Wales, 1063–1415*, Oxford, 1991, p. 462.

5 Throughout most of England at this time, the eldest son inherited his father's property by right (primogeniture). In Wales, and some small areas of England, property was divided equally between all sons. This was the practice known as 'gavelkind'.

6 Henry, fourth earl of Northumberland, met his death in a riot in the Vale of York when he was tax-collecting for Henry VII in 1489.

7 F. W. Brooks, *The Council of the North*, Historical Association pamphlet, London, 1953.

8 J. R. Lander, *Government and community: England, 1450–1509*, London, 1980.

9 See, for example, in addition to the books in the Select bibliography, the detailed account in S. Ellis, *Tudor Ireland, 1470–1603*, London, 1985.

10 For greater detail on the 'Rental' see Ellis, *Tudor Ireland*, Chapter 4; and for a re-examination of early Tudor policy in Ireland see B. Bradshaw, *The Irish constitutional revolution of the sixteenth century*, Cambridge, 1979.

11 Irish parliaments were subject to the English parliament under complex procedures generally summed up in the celebrated Poynings' Law (1494–95). For a detailed discussion see the works of Ellis, *Tudor Ireland* and Bradshaw, *The Irish constitutional revolution*.

4 Henry VIII: 1509–1547

A contemporary portrait of Henry VIII painted by an unknown artist (English School, sixteenth century, c. 1525–30, panel). In what ways could Henry VIII be said to be a typical ruler of the Renaissance period?

The character of Henry VIII

Henry was born at Greenwich on 28 June 1491, and was 18 years old when he succeeded to the throne in 1509. He died at Westminster on 28 January 1547, in his 56th year. Henry was excellently educated; he could speak French, Italian and Spanish and was proficient in Latin. His book, *Assertio septem sacramentorum* (In defence of the seven sacraments), written against Luther in 1521, was almost wholly his own work and proved him to be a competent theologian. In the following year, as a result, Pope Leo X granted Henry the title of *Fidei Defensor* (Defender of the Faith). According to the Venetian ambassadors, the young Henry was an accomplished musician, playing the lute, harpsichord and organ, and according to them he 'acquitted himself divinely' as a dancer. The new king was above average height and excelled also in all manly sports – jousting, riding, archery, hunting and tennis. In temperament Henry was generous – but with occasional meanness – hot-tempered, a lover of luxury and display and in personal morality Henry was no better nor worse than Charles V or Francis I. In fact, Henry VIII was, above all, a Renaissance prince and in his early life the idol of the English nation.

Henry married his dead brother's wife, Catherine of Aragon in 1509. After the birth of her child, Mary, in 1516 it became clear she would have no further children. The Tudor nightmare, the lack of a male heir, began to loom large as Catherine's seven children by Henry (including four sons) did not live. Only the Princess Mary survived. The search for other means to provide a male heir entailed to some extent the break from Rome, and involved considerations of foreign policy, as well as the rise and fall of Cardinal Wolsey and Thomas Cromwell. It is perhaps too simplistic to interpret all of these movements in terms of Henry's motives and personality alone; the political and religious ethos of the age must also be taken into account. Unlike his father, Henry VIII was content to leave the more tedious details of government administration in the hands of his friend and chief minister, Cardinal Thomas Wolsey. Yet Henry was at no time a mere cipher in the politics of the age.

Renaissance England

At this time, England was much influenced by the continental Renaissance, with its emphasis on the revival of ancient Greek and Latin texts and the emergence of new spirit of inquiry in the arts and sciences, which led to a new appreciation of man's place and purpose in the universe. Though the Italian Renaissance was mainly secular and humanistic, in England, under such representative scholars as More, Colet, Linacre, Grocyn and Lily, the English Renaissance was more religious. Much of their scholarship, though not all, went towards translations and re-interpretations of the Bible through the study of its original languages, especially the Greek of the New Testament.

From this group emerged the Oxford Reformers, whose works became widespread because of the newly invented printing press. They were critical of both secular and monastic abuses in the church, but how far they prepared the way for the later Reformation is still a matter of historical controversy. None of these reformers wanted the break up of the church. Yet their anti-clericalism and their attacks on the wealth and privileges of the higher clergy struck a chord of revolt with many in the realm.

There had always been an element of resistance against papal interference in England since the late Middle Ages. The popes of the period were Renaissance princes, more interested in political power and territorial gains in Italy than in their spiritual functions. Luther's attack on the papacy also had an influence in England. Cambridge scholars, such as Tyndale, Latimer and Coverdale, were attracted by some of Luther's ideas, especially by the concept of the subordination of church to state and his appeals to the secular princes to be the instruments of reform in the church.

Henry VIII had no sympathy with these ideas as yet, but they would provide him with useful precedents. Religion and politics were always inextricably mixed, as church and state were united in a commonweal or society. With the reform movements of the sixteenth century, however, the age-old unity of Christendom would break up under emergent nationalism.

Cardinal Wolsey

After the king, Wolsey was the most powerful individual in England. As Lord Chancellor (the king's chief minister) he controlled the whole bureaucratic machinery of government, which Henry VII had so efficiently set up and run, and placed on a sound financial basis. As, moreover, the whole internal government of the realm came under the Lord Chancellor's authority, Wolsey's power extended over the council, the courts, especially the Prerogative ones of Star Chamber, and Requests, as well as the Council in the Marches of Wales and the Council of the North. But as cardinal, papal 'legate a latere' and holder of a vast number of ecclesiastical offices, Wolsey was supreme over the church in England. He exercised all the powers of the pope in England and, in fact, he aspired to the papacy itself. No wonder contemporaries regarded him with awe and believed he had greater powers than the king, since he combined both secular and ecclesiastical powers in his person. Perhaps this unique position was a lesson to Henry VIII of how successful a combination of church and state under royal supremacy could be. And yet the speed and finality of his fall in 1529, at the king's will, is a measure of the reality of royal power in the hands of Henry VIII.[1]

For 15 years, the focus and springboard for Wolsey's administration was the council, but he marginalised its inner circle by concentrating its powers in himself. In effect, he was the council, and in these early years of the reign the king appears to have been ignorant of the details of policy. Wolsey treated parliament with contempt, but then expected it to finance his foreign affairs; he called it twice but had to then rely on the misnamed Benevolences or non-parliamentary taxation. Between 1514 and 1529, Wolsey was virtually master of the realm, and possibly the richest man of his time.[2] Hampton Court Palace was built for him and his household of about 500, but he eventually gave it to Henry in a fruitless effort to regain his favour.

Both the king and his Chancellor were alike in that they were active, ambitious and ostentatious, but different in that Wolsey was meticulous and worked harder than Henry. The volume of work transacted during his chancellorship, especially in the judiciary, was phenomenal. Under him, justice was swift, fines heavy and none could afford to flout the Star Chamber and Court of Requests. By means of these courts, he sought to reduce exploitation of the poor by the rich. He began a great commission of enquiry into the problems created by enclosures, but only succeeded in raising the ire of the landed nobility in currying popular favour. But his own personal lavish display of wealth was at odds with his philanthropic intentions. Wolsey projected more reforms in both church and in the country at large than he ever carried through and, at his departure, the machinery of government and administration was not substantially altered or reformed. Despite his vast power in the church, he did not reform the abuses; his greed and worldliness were hardly a good example to the clergy or laity. As bishop of Bath and Wells, Durham, Winchester, Lincoln, archbishop of York, abbot of St Albans, as well as cardinal and papal legate, together with holding a string of lesser ecclesiastical offices, Wolsey could hardly set about suppressing pluralism and avarice, not to mention preaching holy poverty. His illegitimate son held 11 church offices and their incomes while still a boy. Naturally his ever growing wealth – an income of probably £700,000 per annum in late twentieth-century terms – brought him many envious enemies among the king's friends.

Foreign policy: Wolsey and the king

When Henry came to the throne in 1509, the kings of France and Spain were in conflict over supremacy in Europe, and particularly in Italy which became their battlefield. Unlike his father, Henry VIII began by making war – but war did not bring him the glory and rewards he wanted. Henry embarked on a programme of naval expansion; he had the *Great Harry* built, the finest and largest warship of the age, and a fleet which commanded the English Channel. Meanwhile, Wolsey busied himself building up a diplomatic service of couriers and correspondents all over Europe; and in this he had the services of many scholars of the New Learning at Oxford. Men of the calibre of Richard Pace, John Clerk and Richard Sampson collected and recorded events, details of the size and movements of armies, ships, news of rebellions, gossip from the College of Cardinals, what taxes were being levied in France especially – all the myriad items of business that make up the *State papers foreign*.[3]

Wolsey is best remembered for his conduct of foreign affairs, which caused much controversy at the time and among historians ever since. In any overview of Wolsey's and Henry's foreign policies, it is clear that their actions were not always consistent; but as statesmen they rank high. It has been suggested by some historians that Wolsey, in fact, invented the notion of the 'balance of power'.

The Spanish alliance

Wolsey first allied England with Spain. Henry was clearly resentful of the power of France and would be particularly jealous of its new king, Francis I (1515–47), also a magnificent Renaissance prince. Other factors influencing this decision were that Spain controlled the all important Netherlands wool markets on which England depended for the sale of her broadcloth and, moreover, France was allied to Scotland in the 'Auld Alliance'.

England won an important battle in France in 1513, the army organised by Wolsey but under the command of Henry himself. The ensuing victory, nicknamed the 'Battle of the Spurs', which led to the capture of Tournai, brought Wolsey the bishoprics of Tournai and Lincoln on Henry's request to the pope. These were awards made by the church for military service, for bishops were still expected to be officers of state and, in Wolsey's view, government was too important to be left to laymen.

Meanwhile, Scotland, allied to France, invaded England, but under murderous volleys from the English archers the main army was defeated and the Scottish king, James IV, killed at Flodden Field on 9 September 1513. In the all important peace conference in 1515 between France and Spain, Wolsey acted as mediator.

In 1520, Wolsey organised an alliance with France in the celebrated Field of the Cloth of Gold, perhaps his greatest achievement in foreign policy. But, a few months previously, King Charles of Spain had been elected as Holy Roman Emperor (an election which eluded Henry VIII and which he greatly desired). The Habsburgs once again became predominant in Europe. In 1521, Wolsey, therefore, lost no time in allying England with Spain and the emperor against France once more – a policy that continued until the overwhelming defeat of France at the Battle of Pavia in 1525 and, indeed, until a new alliance was made with France in 1527.

It is clear that Wolsey supported Spain while it was the stronger power. Did Wolsey then also support the policy of the pope (who was on the side of Spain) in the hope that he would be elected to the papacy himself? Some biographers suggest as much, for from 1512 to 1518 England fought France at the behest of the papacy. And did Charles V, the emperor, offer Wolsey the papacy on the death of Leo X, when Wolsey dropped the French alliance in 1521? Perhaps it is best to regard English foreign policy in this reign as the victim of circumstances. Both France and Spain were that much stronger and evenly balanced; hence both courted the English alliance. In the end, Charles V won control of Italy so that the pope became 'an Imperial chaplain'. The final result of Wolsey's foreign policy was to increase the power of Spain at the expense of France without bringing him the papacy. But when Spain and France made peace at Cambrai in 1529, England was not consulted; this was a measure of Wolsey's ultimate failure.

The divorce

The collapse of Wolsey's foreign policy was, however, also tied up with his king's marital and succession problems. In despair for a legitimate male heir, Henry sought a divorce from Catherine of Aragon and entrusted Wolsey with the delicate negotiations with the pope, who alone could grant this request.[4] But, in 1529, the pope was the prisoner of Catherine's nephew, the Emperor Charles V, Wolsey's former ally. The king made Wolsey the scapegoat because of the pope's refusal to grant him a divorce; henceforth, Henry VIII would be his own master. Henry summoned Wolsey before the Court of King's Bench; he avoided trial by pleading guilty and threw himself on the king's mercy, but was dismissed from office as his enemies had convinced the king that the cardinal had betrayed him. Wolsey was ordered to return to London from York, where he had retreated broken in health and spirit. He got as far as Leicester Abbey, where he died in November 1530, reputedly reciting from a psalm 'if I had served God as diligently as I have done the king, he would not have given me over in my grey hairs.'

Wolsey's achievements

Christ Church, Oxford, and Hampton Court Palace are Wolsey's only remaining legacies. In diplomacy, his work was ephemeral. The church in England became transformed by the break with Rome and the ensuing Protestant reforms. The great office of Chancellor went into decline after his day, and the institution that he treated with contempt, parliament, grew in importance, although under the royal will, in Henry's time. Wolsey's contemporary biographer, Cavendish, records, 'that his life was spent in great wealth, joy, triumph and glory'; later historians consider his career a failure.[5]

The royal supremacy and the Reformation

Wolsey's failure to get the pope to agree to a divorce marked, in effect, the beginning of the English Reformation. By 1534, it would end in the denial of papal authority in England, and by declaration of parliament make Henry VIII the Supreme Head of the church in England – a royal supremacy, therefore, over church and state. Henry became an autocrat in the church, but paradoxically gained this position by using parliament, then in a bitterly anti-clerical mood. In its sessions from 1529 until 1536, the first stages of the English Reformation took place. There was no change in doctrine. With the help of his new minister, Thomas Cromwell, Henry still hoped to persuade the pope to grant a divorce by means of threats and parliamentary legislation in the first series of acts from 1529 to 1532 which aimed at removing clerical abuse.

The breach with Rome

The second stage, 1532 to 1533, marks the actual breach with Rome and the pope. Anne Boleyn was expecting a child in 1533, and for it to be a legitimate heir the divorce and the re-marriage of the king had to be hastened. Thomas Cromwell took the Henrician Reformation to its logical conclusion – the king's supremacy over the church. Cromwell ensured the passage of the celebrated Act in Restraint of Appeals (1533), which stated that all 'spiritual cases' dealing with marriages, wills, tithes were to be settled in England, and this had the effect of taking the royal divorce case out of the pope's jurisdiction. Thomas Cranmer was sympathetic to the king's plight and was rewarded with the archbishopric of Canterbury. Cranmer divorced Henry from Catherine and married him to Anne (May–June 1533). The Act in Restraint of Appeals, furthermore, laid it down that 'this realm of England is an empire . . . governed by one Supreme Head and king', and, in this way, the royal supremacy was legally established and papal authority eliminated. An Act of Succession followed to ensure that the children of Anne and Henry would succeed to the throne.[6] The acts establishing the succession and the royal supremacy were then re-inforced by the Treasons Act, virtually making all opposition to these changes punishable as treason.

By the end of 1535, all subjects were required to take an oath accepting the Acts of Succession and Supremacy; it was their refusal to take this oath which produced the first martyrs of the Henrician Reformation. Sir Thomas More, John

Thomas Cromwell, Henry VIII's chief minister from 1532 to 1540, wearing the Order of St George (from the School of Hans Holbein (1497–1543)). How many of Cromwell's reforms survived the death of Henry VIII?

Fisher and the Carthusian monks of the London Charterhouse went to the block before the end of 1535. It is significant that More refused to answer the question when asked if Henry was head of the church, arguing that there was no law which made silence an offence. Eventually, under pressure, probably from Cromwell, Richard Rich, an old acquaintance of More's, committed perjury and swore that More had denied that parliament could make Henry head of the church. In his final speech after conviction, More boldly asserted that no layman could be head of the church.

Thomas Cromwell's achievements

Thomas Cromwell's ideas and achievements between 1532 and 1540 as the king's chief minister have all come under scrutiny. Among the many questions raised are: What part did Cromwell play in the break with Rome? Did he manipulate and manage parliament? How did he control its composition? What attempts did he make to influence it in favour of the king's wishes? To what extent was he responsible for the destruction of the monasteries? Elton describes Cromwell's handling of English government as 'revolutionary' in that he supervised the emergence of a new monarchy based on parliament and working through bureaucratic institutions which had a life of their own. But, how many of the Cromwellian administrative reforms survived the death of Henry?

The Reformation Parliament

The importance of the Reformation Parliament needs some qualification in the light of research since the 1960s. In the unprecedented length of its sittings, and in the importance of the legislation it was required to pass, the Reformation Parliament was unique. Henry VIII's deliberate decision to take the nation into partnership in his use of parliament needs to be qualified. Parliament did *not* make the royal supremacy – that was the work of the king and Cromwell; they *used* parliament to give the sanction of the common law of England to their actions. In a word, parliament *legalised* the Reformation. At this stage, the king was always in control, the senior partner; he had no reason to fear any increase in the power of the Commons, even though they did not always accept all his policies without question. But, after 1529, the crown extended its own influence over elections to the Commons and put privy councillors in the Commons to look after its interests there.

The state of the church

The so-called 'decadence' of the church needs some qualification. The work of A. G. Dickens, and that of C. Haigh, E. Duffy and others, shows that the church in England on the eve of the Reformation was by no means moribund. There were of course worldly and wealthy prelates – pluralists, like Wolsey; there were many ignorant and hidebound priests, lacking in celibacy – all of which gave impetus to the native anti-clerical tradition dating from Wycliffe and the Lollards, which was fanned into action by the new Protestant influences from the continent. The church in England was, therefore, in a real sense, ripe for reform.

The dissolution of the monasteries

There is no doubt that the monastic houses were in decline, but it is likely that the real reason for their dissolution was financial. The crown was the chief beneficiary from the resulting land transfer, the greatest since the Norman Conquest. Henry had, however, to resell two-thirds of the monastic properties to meet debts and the needs of patronage, so that the country gentlemen benefited and became a powerful sector of the commonweal. Queen Mary Tudor found this out to her cost, since they now had a vested interest in the maintenance of the Reformation.

The Pilgrimage of Grace

A more immediate result of the dissolution was the rebellion in 1536 known as the Pilgrimage of Grace. Why did it break out and what did it achieve? Why was the crown able to break this formidable revolt so easily and so rapidly?

The rebellion was the most serious insurrection of the common people to take place in England between the Peasants' Revolt of 1381 and the Civil War of the 1640s. Nine rebel armies mobilised in the North, especially in Lincolnshire and Yorkshire, in October 1536. Recent research stresses that the insurgents' aim was as much to safeguard the common land from enclosure as it was to protect Christ's faith; and that therefore, the Pilgrimage of Grace cannot be fully explained as a simple reaction to the Henrician Reformation. However, it was not a purely popular rising but rather an amalgamation of protests from gentry, clergy and commons working together against the government. Among their demands was the repeal of the Statute of Uses, which prevented landowners from bequeathing their lands to trusts (to avoid paying death duties), the removal of Thomas Cromwell from power, an end to monastic dissolutions, the restoration of the pope, and of Mary Tudor to the royal succession. The king made concessions, promising to pardon all but ten of the ringleaders and to discuss their demands in parliament and to compromise on the restoration of the abbeys. With the submission of Robert Aske, the major leader of the rebels, at Doncaster, the revolt was virtually over. The rebellion in 1537, under Sir Francis Bigod in east Yorkshire, was brutally crushed by the duke of Norfolk for the king. Henry had won: he had stood by Cromwell and the bishops and he neither ratified nor repudiated the terms agreed with the rebels. And so ended the largest popular revolt in England, and, perhaps, the greatest crisis of Henry's reign.

The execution of Anne Boleyn

The Henrician Reformation began with the fall of Wolsey; it was hastened on by the birth of Elizabeth on 7 September 1533. When Anne's second child was stillborn, Henry was already in love with Jane Seymour and the problem of a male heir was no nearer solution. Catherine of Aragon died in 1536, on the same day as Anne's second child. Within four months, Anne was executed for crimes of infidelity which the prosecutors could not prove. Her successor, Jane Seymour, gave Henry the son he wanted in October 1537, but she died after giving birth.

For the next decade, the Seymours were greatly favoured by the king and their rise would see the fall of the king's second great minister, Thomas Cromwell.

The fall of Thomas Cromwell

Cromwell wanted to cement a Protestant alliance with Cleves and proposed Anne as Henry's next queen. The marriage with Anne of Cleves only lasted six months; she was awarded a handsome divorce settlement. Meantime Bishop Gardiner and the duke of Norfolk promoted Catherine Howard at court to be a Catholic rival to the German Protestant circle around Cromwell and Anne of Cleves. Henry married for the fifth time in July 1540. His bride was Catherine Howard, niece of that duke of Norfolk who had led the assault on Cromwell. By November 1541, rumours of the new queen's indiscretions and misdemeanours brought her to the executioner's block before she had borne any children to Henry. In 1543, Henry married for the last time. His new queen was Catherine Parr, who survived him by less than two years; there were no children by this marriage.

Henry VIII's last years

In the last years of the reign, foreign policy became complicated by the religious changes: as long as France and Spain were at war Henry was safe; when both were at peace, England was open to attack from either France or Spain in the interests of the papacy. This is why Cromwell urged the Protestant alliance which ultimately cost him his life in 1540. Henry found his council divided in the final years between the conservative Catholic Howard element and the new Protestant interest surrounding Thomas Cranmer, the archbishop of Canterbury. Henry strove for a compromise, saving Cranmer from charges of heresy on three occasions between 1543 and 1545. Henry promoted the new vernacular liturgy and the English Bible. But, by the Six Articles of 1539, Transubstantiation[7] was a required doctrine under pain of death. The penalties were removed the following year from the 'whip with six strings' as the act came to be called. Henry stuck to orthodox Catholic teaching, save on the papacy, and this was enshrined in *The necessary doctrine and erudition of any Christian man* (May 1543), known as the 'King's Book'. Henry was in complete control of the church, but he wished to act prudently and preserve religious unity throughout the realm.

Henry VIII and Wales

Law and order was breaking down in Wales and in the Marches. Welsh support was necessary for the revolution in church and state that was going forward between 1529 and 1536. Thomas Cromwell was especially active in restoring good government in Wales, for example all felons were to be prevented from crossing the Severn to or from south Wales and the Forest of Dean. Another act was passed to ensure that juries would convict the guilty. Previously many sheriffs had experienced difficulties in both summoning juries and in persuading them to return guilty verdicts when appropriate. Constitutionally this was the most important act to bring the administration of the Welsh shires into line with that of England. In 1536, the Act of Union was passed, whereby all Welsh peoples became citizens of the new kingdom of England and Wales. In effect, English law, administration, the English language and customs were to be extended to all Wales, and the former Principality was to send representatives to the English parliament. A final act of 1543 completely assimilated Wales to England. But the progress of the Reformation in Wales was slow, and this is largely explained by the usual conservative obstruction to the new religion found in any provincial area in any part of Europe. Another factor was that Wales was 90 per cent Welsh speaking throughout all the changes in England, and this figure was little altered by the middle of the next century. Wales did eventually become Protestant, but at its own pace and in its own language, and without much disruption of its local ruling class.

Henry VIII and Ireland

Henry VIII was less suspicious of his overmighty subjects than his father had been. In Ireland, the ninth earl of Kildare, Gearóid Óg, had to suffer more direct interference from the king than had his father and more competition from the Butlers, the earls of Ormonde, with whom the Fitzgeralds had feuded for centuries. Henry began to use Irish offices as rewards for his courtiers such as the appointment of John Kite as archbishop of Armagh in 1514 and the admission to court of Sir Thomas Boleyn. He would rise ever higher as Henry became involved with his daughters Mary and Anne – the latter to be queen and mother to the future Elizabeth I. In Ireland itself, the claims of the Boleyns to the Ormonde inheritance would make them serious rivals to the Kildares.

Growing criticisms of Kildare led to his summons to England to answer a series of charges in 1518 and 1519; as usual, Kildare took a year to reply, but that delay hastened the debate on how 'Ireland might be reduced to good order and obedience'. The upshot was that Kildare was replaced as chief Governor by an English nobleman, Thomas Howard, earl of Surrey, the future duke of Norfolk. Wolsey and Kildare had a fierce dispute in the council. Kildare was retained at court and Surrey arrived in Ireland in May 1520 with an army; his commission was nothing less than the restoration of the royal authority over the whole island.

In his instructions to Surrey, Henry made it obvious that he was unwilling to spend money on Ireland simply to achieve the mere outward obedience of the Gaelic lords. Recognition of the royal authority had to be accompanied by a willingness to accept the rule of law and to keep only those lands to which they were legally entitled. Conformity to the English model could, however, contain approved elements of their own Brehon law system (the customary system of law and practice of the Gaelic Irish).

This compromise caused much trouble later, as Irish land law, based on the family or kin, was at odds with English land law based on primogeniture. Dispossession and re-distribution of lands took place after rebellions, perpetuating feuds and revolts during the rest of the sixteenth century. Henry VIII's aim in Ireland was to proceed 'by sober ways, politic drifts and amiable persuasions'; Surrey was to avoid force, use diplomacy and duplicity to win over the Gaelic Irish. According to Ellis, 'the earl of Surrey's lieutenancy (1520–22) originated in one of Henry VIII's spasmodic fits of reforming energy'.[8] Surrey was kept short of men and money and he once pointed out to Henry that his predecessor Edward I had spent ten years on the conquest of Wales, and Ireland was five times the size of Wales and separated by the sea from England. The reduction of Ireland, therefore, would take at least ten years and would need an influx of English settlers to secure the military conquests. Surrey's expedition had already cost about £13,000; it served to break the power of Kildare in the king's eyes and the appointment of Piers Butler, earl of Ormonde, to succeed Surrey in 1522 shifted the reliance of the crown on the Kildares to their rivals, the Ormondes. They could draw on Irish resources as the Kildares had done to rule Ireland for the crown; aristocratic delegation still proved to be the cheapest way to govern Ireland in the period.

Kildare's reconciliation with the king, however, and his marriage to the daughter of the marquis of Dorset led to a change in Henry's Irish policy and, in August 1524, Kildare was re-appointed Lord Deputy of Ireland. Butler, earl of Ormonde, was to be made Treasurer. Such a compromise, however, became impossible; Henry had to summon both Kildare and Ormonde to England in 1526. In their absence, disorder broke out in Ireland. It was at this stage that Henry appointed his illegitimate son Henry, duke of Richmond, as an absentee lieutenant to carry out with a group of officials the government of Ireland. It was called a 'secret council' but it proved useless, and in 1530 Henry appointed Sir William Skeffington as Lord Deputy. Kildare refused to co-operate with him and by the summer of 1532 the wheel turned full circle with the re-instatement of Kildare as chief Governor.

Clearly there had been no satisfactory solution other than aristocratic delegation in the government of Ireland. The re-appointment of Kildare coincided with Henry's efforts to gain his divorce from Catherine and to shake off the jurisdiction of the papacy. Furthermore, Thomas Cromwell began to interfere in the Irish administration by securing the appointment of officials loyal to himself rather than to Kildare – the latter began to make arrangements against his own dismissal. In February 1534, he had to appear again at court. In his absence, he had appointed his son, Silken Thomas, as Vice Deputy, since Skeffington's appointment to the post had not been finalised until May 1534. But, in June, Silken Thomas, after the premature report of his father's death in the Tower, repudiated his allegiance to Henry VIII. This led inexorably on to the arrest of his father, who died in the Tower in September. Dublin was besieged, Archbishop Alen murdered, and the rebellion spread throughout the Pale. By March 1535, royal forces under 'Gunner' Skeffington, as he became known for his use of ordnance in the siege and capture of Maynooth Castle, captured the head-quarters of Kildare's military power. Kildare eventually surrendered by August. Kildare and his five uncles were executed at Tyburn in February 1537.

In the previous year, the Reformation acts of parliament were passed in Dublin and George Browne consecrated archbishop of Dublin at Lambeth Palace. By 1539, the legal Reformation of the Irish church was complete with the surrender of the monasteries. By a policy known as 'Surrender and Re-grant' many of the Gaelic leaders took English titles in submission to the king's wishes. In return, they were to receive their ancestral lands back from the king, hold them like their English counterparts in return for knight service, and pass them on to their eldest sons under English laws of inheritance. The policy was only half-heartedly put into practice, mainly because Irish lands belonged to the kin and not to the person elected to head the family.

Sir Anthony St Leger, as the new Lord Deputy, promoted this new direction in Irish policy, favouring conciliation by 'surrender and regrant', rather than coercion, in the hope that he would win the co-operation of the Irish lords with crown authority. In June 1541, by act of the Irish parliament, the ancient medieval Lordship of Ireland whereby English monarchs were 'Lords of Ireland' was formally and constitutionally changed by declaring Henry VIII king of Ireland.[9]

The pious hope was that the sister kingdom would live in harmony with all its peoples – Gaelic Irish, Old and New English and under the English monarch, albeit an absentee one. The subsequent history of Ireland tells a different story. Henceforth, Tudor policies for Ireland fluctuated between plans for conquest and colonisation and various conciliatory schemes, financially less exacting than conquest.

Henry VIII and the kingdom of Scotland

In the first half of the sixteenth century, Scotland was largely a client state of France. Henry VIII's war with France and Scotland from 1512 to 1514 brought financial exhaustion and the appearance of victory at Flodden in Scotland against James IV (1488–1513) and Tournai in France. Flodden Field in 1513 was a massacre, for Scotland lost her king, nine earls, thirteen lords and one or more members of every important family in the land. Thousands of 'mere folk' died; according to English records, 10,000 Scots were killed and 1,500 English. In Scotland, the battle was seldom mentioned by name and, in England, it was sometimes regarded as the revenge for the Battle of Bannockburn fought on 24 June 1314, near Stirling. But for 30 years after Flodden, the English monarchy still found it difficult to exercise political authority in the lowlands of Scotland.

With an infant king, James V (1513–42), who was only one year old when he came to the throne, Scotland was strongly influenced by European events such as the rivalry between Francis I and Charles V, the Lutheran Reformation and Henry VIII's break with Rome. England, France, the emperor and the papacy all courted Scotland's friendship and support. This created divisions among the Scottish nobility. At 18 years old, James V's personal rule became marked by energetic action against the disorders of the nobles, especially in Argyll and the Isles, and by his exploitation and extortion of the church's revenues, despite his determination to maintain Catholicism. He had inherited a kingdom bankrupted by his mother, Margaret Tudor, and her second husband, the earl of Angus. His marriage to Madeleine, the eldest daughter of Francis I, in January 1537 was short-lived; she died after eight weeks in Scotland on 7 July 1537. His second marriage in June 1538 to Mary, the daughter of the duke of Guise, was intended to continue the French alliance and maintain Catholicism.

The marriage, however, aroused Henry VIII's fears of encirclement by a league of Roman Catholic powers; he was after all denounced by them as a heretic, adulterer, and despoiler of the church.[10] Henry VIII was James V's uncle and at one stage Henry offered him Mary Tudor as his bride. She was refused, as James simply saw the offer as yet another ploy on the part of his uncle to further English claims of suzerainty to the Scottish kingdom. Furthermore, when Henry invited James to a meeting at York in September 1541 to reach an agreement, the Scottish privy council dissuaded James from attending. Henry waited at York without meeting either the Scottish king, or his emissary. Henry, in his anger, let loose the northern levies to cross the border in a vicious campaign of burning and looting in the 1540s which became known as 'the rough wooing'. The check of the English forces by the earl of Home at Haddonrig in August 1542 was only temporary. James's queen, Mary, was awaiting the birth of an heir. On 24 November 1542, the Scots army was put to a disorderly rout at Solway Moss near the River Esk. John Knox, the zealous reformer, saw the hand of God as a just punishment in the defeat. The military defeat and the news in early December 1542 of the birth of his daughter, the future Mary, queen of Scots, hastened King James V's end. He is supposed to have remarked, 'Adieu, farewell, it came with a lass, it will pass with a lass.'[11]

When James V died on the 14 December 1542, Mary, now queen of Scots, was one week old. Henry VIII began negotiations for her marriage with his son Edward, then aged five, but these were frustrated by the Catholic party under Cardinal Beaton in Scotland. Henry wanted Mary to be brought up at the English court after she was ten years old. The treaty at Greenwich in July 1543, at which these arrangements were made, was overtaken by internal events in Scotland, especially the coronation of Mary at nine months old in Stirling Castle on 9 September 1543. The pro-English party among the nobility stayed away. Inauspiciously, the date was the thirtieth anniversary of Flodden Field. But the direction of Scottish affairs by the English monarch, either through diplomacy or bullying, receded with the renewal of the French alliance.

Meanwhile, Mary was despatched to France for safety; there she remained until she was nineteen, according to Knox 'sold to the devil . . . for a plague to this realm and for her final destruction'. English raids continued to exert a stranglehold on south-eastern Scotland. French military aid arrived in Scotland by December 1547 (fifty captains) and, in June 1548, a force of 6,000 under André de Montalembert. The Scottish parliament at Edinburgh assented to the marriage of Mary to Francis the dauphin of France in July 1548. The conditions were that the king of France should defend Scotland as he did his own realm, but that he should respect Scotland's independence.

What would be the outcome in Scotland's history when Mary returned to rule? She was queen of a country she did not know. She was also married to a weak and sickly husband, the heir to the French throne. She could well combine the two kingdoms of France and Scotland. And the throne of England could well pass to Mary as the legitimate descendant of Henry VIII's elder sister Margaret, declaring, as she did, that Elizabeth was illegitimate.

In 1556, the same year that Mary married Francis, Mary Tudor died and her half-sister, Elizabeth, came to the English throne. The outbreak of the wars of religion in France would open the way for Elizabeth to support the pro-English element in Scotland when the balance would turn in favour of the Protestant Reformation in the Scottish lowlands.

Document case study

Henry VIII

4.1 The king's appearance and accomplishments

P. Pasqualigo, a Venetian diplomat, in a dispatch of 1515

His Majesty is the handsomest potentate I ever set eyes on; above the usual height, with an extremely fine calf to his leg, his complexion very fair and bright, auburn hair combed straight and short, in the French fashion, and a round face so very beautiful that it would become a pretty woman, his throat being rather long and thick . . . He will enter his twenty-fifth year the month after next. He speaks French, English and Latin, and a little Italian, plays well on the lute and harpsichord, sings from book at sight, draws the bow with greater strength than any man in England and jousts marvellously . . . a most accomplished Prince.

Source: J. Brewer, J. Gairdner and J. Brodie, (eds.) *Letters and papers of Henry VIII*, vol. 2, London, 1862–1910, p. 395

4.2 Henry's friendship with Sir Thomas More

The words of William Roper, More's son-in-law

And for the pleasure he took in company, would his grace suddenly times come home to his house at Chelsea, to be merry with him, whither on a time unlooked for, he came to dinner to him; and after dinner, in a fair garden of his, walked with him by the space of an hour, holding his arm about his neck . . . as I have never seen him do to any other except Cardinal Wolsey.

Source: William Roper, *The lyfe of Sir Thomas Moore, knight*, ed. by E. V. Hitchcock, London, 1935

4.3 Impressions of Henry's court in the 1540s

The French ambassador to Montmorency, 1540 (letter)

. . . they make of him not only a king to be obeyed but an idol to be worshipped. Thus a climax of evils has arisen . . . in England. This Prince seems tainted, among other vices, which in a king may be called plagues. The first is that he is so covetous that all the riches in the world would not satisfy him . . . thence proceeds the second plague, distrust and fear . . . he will not cease to dip his hand in blood as long as he doubts his people . . . and the third plague, lightness and inconstancy proceeds partly from the other two and partly from the nature of the nation which has perverted the rights of religion.

Source: J. Brewer, J. Gairdner and J. Brodie, (eds.) *Letters and papers of Henry VIII*, London, 1862–1910, 15, 954

4.4 The position of parliament in Henry VIII's reign

The view of a modern historian

By the beginning of the sixteenth century, therefore, Parliament was a regular institution, with recognised powers and functions. It was superior to similar institutions elsewhere because it had no rivals in regional assemblies, because it genuinely provided an opportunity for all political interests to argue and resolve their conflicts, because it was quite exceptionally organised for business, and because (all these facts combining) it not only participated in government but was positively useful to the monarchy.

Source: G. R. Elton, 'Parliament: the whole body of the realm', in *Studies in Tudor and Stuart politics and government*, vol. 2, Cambridge, 1974, p. 50

4.5 Henry VIII's personal possessions

Henry VIII's inventory of personal possessions runs to four volumes of listings. Dr Starkey, a historian who is transcribing and editing these volumes, makes the following comments

Henry had an income of £300,000 a year when the next wealthiest people in the land had incomes of £6000 a year and the average daily wage was 2.5 pence. The index of these volumes covers more than 100,000 personal items. All that the King owned when he died in 1547 was fastidiously listed on the finest linen paper by an army of scribes. He was the original shopaholic. Everything was bought, and bought in quantity, and everything was bought to be used to give the impression of wealth.

The list begins: '1 item; the king's crown of gold'. Some of the items came from the dissolution of the monasteries, but much more from the enemies he destroyed, such as Wolsey, the Dukes of Buckingham and Norfolk . . .

Source: *The Times*, 20 January 1997

4.6 Henry's achievements as monarch

J. J. Scarisbrick wrote an influential modern biography of Henry VIII; he concludes with this assessment of the king

Henry was a huge, consequential and majestic figure. At least for some, he was everything that a people could wish him to be – a bluff, confident patriot king who was master of his kingdom and feared no one. By the end of his long reign, despite everything, he was indisputably revered, indeed, in some strange way, loved. He had raised monarchy to near idolatry. He had become the quintessence of Englishry and the focus of swelling national pride.

Source: J. J. Scarisbrick, *Henry VIII*, London, 1st edn, 1968, p. 506

Document case-study questions

1 What impression of Henry VIII can be obtained from 4.1, 4.2, 4.5, and 4.6?

2 Document 4.3 is a later source. To what extent is the impression given in 4.3 borne out by the details in 4.5?

3 Why did Elton think parliament under Henry VIII was an important part of government?

4 How much of a contrast can be drawn from all these documents between the early and late years of Henry VIII's reign?

Notes and references

1 A primary source for Wolsey is G. Cavendish, *The life and death of Cardinal Wolsey*, R. S. Sylvester (ed.), London, 1959.

2 Note he was denied the archbishopric of Canterbury – the one major ecclesiastical appointment that eluded him because of the longevity of Archbishop Warham, Wolsey's patron in the early days.

3 For example J. Brewer, J. Gairdner and J. Brodie, (eds.) *Letters and papers, foreign and domestic, of the reign of Henry VIII*, vols. 1–21, London, 1862–1910, with an *Addenda* in 1929–32.

4 Catherine's former marriage to Henry's elder brother Arthur, who died in 1502, put Catherine within the forbidden canonical degrees of kinship to Henry (according to a canon based on Leviticus, xx, 21). Also, see J. Scarisbrick, *Henry VIII*, London, 1968, ch. vii, 'The canon law of the divorce'.

5 Wolsey's reputation has been rehabilitated in P. Gwyn's biography, *The king's cardinal*, London, 1990. The porphyry tomb that he had commissioned to hold his corpse now holds the remains of Lord Nelson in the crypt of St Paul's Cathedral.

6 In the search for a male heir, Henry VIII married six wives. It is often forgotten that he brought out his illegitimate son, Henry Fitzroy, and showered honours on him with a view to nominating him heir. He was made duke of Richmond and Lord Lieutenant of Ireland. At one stage, Henry contemplated marrying him to Mary, his half-sister and only surviving child of Henry VIII and Catherine of Aragon. Fitzroy's mother was Elizabeth Blount; but he died at 17 years old, poisoned, it is rumoured, by Anne Boleyn.

7 Transubstantiation is the belief that Christ's words at the Last Supper spoken by the priest during the service of the Mass change the substance of the bread and wine into the body and blood of Christ.

8 S. Ellis, *Tudor Ireland, 1470–1603*, London, 1985, p. 108.

9 One of the arguments used for the change of title was that 'the Lordship of Ireland' had echoes of the original grant of Ireland by the papacy to the English king Henry II in the twelfth century. Moreover, Silken Thomas's agents to the papacy in December 1534 had stressed that since the king of England ruled Ireland by papal authority, Henry had, by his rejection of the pope, forfeited all right to the land of Ireland.

10 Though officially Catholic, the Scottish church was divided between those wishing for reform of its abuses from within, and those wanting to follow the English example and break away root and branch from the tree of Rome. It was not until the 1560s that the lowlands of Scotland would become Protestant.

11 The historical allusion is to the marriage of Marjorie Bruce and Walter Stuart, the medieval founders of the Stuart dynasty. James V was a false prophet, for the dynasty did not end with Mary Queen of Scots, her son James extended it to both England and Ireland.

Edward VI: 1547–1553

Somerset: Protector of the Realm, 1547–1549

Edward was born at Hampton Court on the 12 October 1537 and died on the 6 July 1553, in his sixteenth year. He was the sole legitimate son of Henry VIII by his third wife Jane Seymour, who died two weeks after Edward's birth. By Henry VIII's last will and testament, a Council of Sixteen, made up of equal members, was to be appointed during the royal minority. Moreover, by the third Succession Act of 1543, the rights of his children, Mary and Elizabeth (though illegitimate), were maintained. By Henry's will of December 1546, the line of succession was to be Edward, Mary and Elizabeth; after them came the collateral heirs to the throne. These were the descendants of Henry's two sisters, Mary, his younger sister, and Margaret of Scotland. Mary's progeny, who were to inherit first, were all girls: Frances, duchess of Suffolk, and her daughters, the three Grey sisters. Then came the descendants of Margaret of Scotland. These were her grandchildren, Mary Queen of Scots and Henry, Lord Darnley. After Edward, all but one of the potential claimants to the English throne were women.

Henry's death on 28 January 1547 was kept secret for three days, while the councillors, Edward Seymour, earl of Hertford and duke of Somerset, and William Paget, veteran of Tudor government and Henry's former diplomat, were busily negotiating. They persuaded the council that it was Henry's real wish not to have collective government by a council of equals, but to make Edward Seymour, his brother-in-law and uncle to the young king, Protector. Seymour became the virtual regent of the realm and took the title duke of Somerset. The other councillors had to be bought off with new lands and titles.

Somerset faced immense problems in every sphere, political, religious, financial, social and economic, that turned the years after 1547 into crisis. The country was divided over religion, at war with Scotland and suffering from a debased coinage with its inevitable result, acute inflation. While Somerset had achieved high standing and popularity under Henry VIII, especially for his military successes at Boulogne and in Scotland, he did not have the capacity or abilities successfully to overcome the problems facing the minority government.

Somerset has been variously judged by historians as an incompetent idealist, inept, and of overweening self-confidence, which despite his high Protestant ideals led him into sharp practices. In the past, he had taken his share of monastic spoils – even to the extent of trying to destroy Westminster Abbey. He had built Somerset House on the Strand out of ruined churches. In fact, Somerset and his followers were moderate Protestants and stood for paternal social reforms, but, because Somerset did not combine enlightened aims with statesman-like methods, he seemed to be incapable of implementing them. Although he was a first-class military man, he put intolerable strains on the treasury by his invasion of Scotland, which in the end only resulted in driving the Scots deeper into the 'Auld Alliance' with France. He did envisage an eventual peaceful union of England and Scotland in 'one empire', planning to symbolise this by the marriage of the boy-king Edward to the child-queen of Scotland, Mary Stuart. However, Somerset's military action, especially the victory at the Battle of Pinkie in September 1547, put an end to the 'rough wooing'. Mary was shipped off to France, eventually to marry the dauphin.

Financial problems

A sound economy has always been a necessary foundation of good government. Thanks to Henry VIII's 'Great Debasement' of the coinage and the dissolution of the monasteries, the crown was wealthy during the 1540s and this enabled Henry and Somerset to spend around £3.5 million on six years of warfare in France and Scotland. But, by 1552, the crown was bankrupt – the Tudors never again had enough wealth to launch major military campaigns on the scale of those of France and Spain.

Debasement and dissolution continued under Edward VI. A rapid price rise was followed by a boom in the export of cloth and wool which, in turn, hastened the enclosure movement. This was accompanied by all kinds of ills: profiteering and increased unemployment, and poverty and distress among the rural peasantry.

Prices, especially of land, went up steeply when a run of bad harvests coincided with setbacks in overseas trade. While the gentry had capital to exploit their opportunities and yeomen and husbandmen could profit from the rise in the price of farm produce the poorer husbandmen and, above all, the cottager class with little or no land became further impoverished. An end to rack renting, fines and the enclosure of common land for deer parks and for sheep would all be found in the demands of the peasantry as they rose in rebellion in the great disturbances of 1549.

Religious change

When Henry died, reforming Protestants were already on the ascendant. Somerset surrounded himself with them and turned out the leading Catholics from his circle. This gained him much popularity in London. William Paget, the ablest of his advisers, felt it necessary to warn Somerset not to put popular Protestantism above the peace of the realm.

Somerset, however, did move cautiously and brought some of the Cambridge reforming school into politics, men of the calibre of William Cecil and Thomas Smith, later to be ministers of note during Elizabeth's reign. Under the direction of Thomas Cranmer, the archbishop of Canterbury, Henry's heresy laws and the Act of the Six Articles were repealed and, as parliament met, London mobs indulged in a frenzy of iconoclasm – breaking church images, whitewashing walls, breaking up altars and selling off vestments to the City tailors. The destruction of paintings and stained-glass windows was encouraged throughout the land by broadsheets. Homilies, published by royal authority, ignored the Mass and the Roman practice of Communion in one kind. An act ordered the administration of the Sacrament to all who so desired in both kinds.[1] Another act swept away the pretence of election of bishops and arranged for their appointment by letters patent issued by the king. Cranmer produced the first Protestant Prayer Book in English and had it enforced by a mild Act of Uniformity in 1549.

The new Chantries Act of 1547 ordered some two thousand chantries, that is chapels in which priests were employed to say Mass for the souls of the dead, and all the properties of all guilds, in so far as they were dedicated to 'superstition and popery', to be confiscated. This caused strong opposition in the Commons and outright rebellion in Cornwall. Foreign scholars from Germany, and Italy like Martin Bucer and Peter Martyr and many supporters of Zwingli from Zurich like Hooper were brought into the universities to educate a new generation of clergy in the reformed doctrines. Royal chaplains began to read all their church services in English. Commissioners visited the universities to give them new statutes, but also encouraged the destruction of images, stained-glass windows and church organs and left them in confusion and disorder. The gulf between Catholicism and the new reformed religion, which became more strongly Protestant, widened; the doctrine of justification by faith alone (rather than by faith *and* good works), together with the concept of God's elect meant a more individualistic religion. The weight put by Catholics on the sacraments and good works was diminished; more stress was put on the vernacular scriptures, services in English and on preaching. Emphasis was placed on the pulpit and the congregation, rather than on the altar and the priest.

The new prayer book, the Book of Common Prayer of 1549, dictated a decidedly Protestant mode of worship. Howard, the duke of Norfolk, and Stephen Gardiner, the bishop of Winchester, although in the Tower, resisted Cranmer and Somerset on principle. They argued that, partly because all these changes were being enforced during the king's minority, supremacy no longer belonged to the king but to the council.

Social policy and rebellion

In 1548, Somerset set up a commission to enquire into the evils resulting from enclosure. This increased his unpopularity with the nobility and led the peasantry to believe that he was on their side. He could not, however, ignore rebellion. The result of the widespread discontent was Kett's 1549 rebellion in Norfolk; the causes, unlike the one in Cornwall of the same year, were largely economic. Hugh Latimer's course of sermons on the iniquities of the times highlighted all that was wrong with the regime. England was ready for rebellion, as the people looked angrily upon a new upstart nobility, fattening on sacrilegious spoils. More importantly, 'strong' government under Henry now contrasted with the rule of a minor; economic depression, high prices, inflationary coinage debasement, religious innovation, social reforms which raised expectations but which failed to deliver results and Somerset's inability to work with the rest of the council all caused resentment. It is not surprising, therefore, that widespread rioting and discontent broke out in Devon, Cornwall, Norfolk, Suffolk, most of the Midland shires and in Yorkshire. In the south-west and East Anglia, the government had to employ full-scale military action in which about 6,000 perished in a series of sieges and battles. The ambitious, unscrupulous earl of Warwick – the future duke of Northumberland, Henry's agent and able military general, and Somerset's successor – took control of putting down the rebellions.

Somerset's fall

In effect, Warwick's crushing of the Norfolk rebels led by Robert Kett, mainly by German mercenaries and Welsh gunners, led to the downfall of Somerset, as his enemies could claim the credit for restoring law and order. During this time, the conspiracy of his own brother, Thomas Seymour, Lord High Admiral, who had married Henry's widow, Catherine Parr, also came to light. Thomas Seymour had hoped to consolidate his power by having Lady Jane Grey marry Edward VI and when Catherine, his wife, died he entertained hopes of marrying the Princess Elizabeth himself. To Somerset such overweening dynastic ambitions amounted to treason, and in January 1549 he disposed of his rival by act of attainder and the block on Tower Hill.

Somerset's own fall was largely due to his inept handling of the rebellions, and that the work of crushing the rebels had been taken over by his even more ruthless rival in the council, John Dudley, earl of Warwick. He was the son of the Dudley who had been the efficient but unpopular servant of Henry VII and who had been executed by Henry VIII, and father of Robert Dudley, the future earl of Leicester, one of Queen Elizabeth's favourites.

Another reason for Somerset's fall was the disastrous consequences of his foreign policy. Because of the Franco-Scottish alliance, his invasion of Scotland finally provoked Henry II of France into declaring war, so that Henry VIII's one conquest, Boulogne, was eventually lost. By the autumn of 1548, French troops were steadily setting about recouping all that the English had held in Scotland.

There were also some signs that a Catholic reaction to the severities of the Edwardian Reformation was about to take place. Therefore, to prevent possible political upheaval, the earl of Warwick quietly moved in to take over the council. He studiously avoided taking the title Protector. Somerset was put in the Tower, but as a reaction in his favour seemed imminent, Warwick, who by now had taken the title duke of Northumberland, had him executed in January 1552 on Tower Hill.

The rule of Northumberland, 1549–1553

John Dudley, earl of Warwick and duke of Northumberland (1502?–1553), soldier, sailor and statesman, dominated the second half of Edward VI's reign. He was feared and envied; his three years of power displayed to the full the ambitious rapacity of the nobility. As lord lieutenant of the army under Somerset, his forces had ravaged the lowlands of Scotland and burnt out Edinburgh and, in 1547, had decisively defeated the Scots at Pinkie. As President of the Council of Wales, he had recruited heavily there for the army for the wars against France and Scotland. He had also taken over the suppression of Kett's Rebellion.

Religion

Doctrinal reformation led to further confiscations of church properties and newly appointed bishops were made to pay for their consecrations with episcopal property. For example, the see of Gloucester was suppressed and Durham 'refounded' which resulted in substantial gifts to Northumberland. He was a great deal more corrupt than Somerset, certainly more ruthless, lacking in personal religious conviction and without Somerset's high ideals. He soon identified with the more extreme Protestant elements. Parliament's approval of a Second Book of Common Prayer heralded a much more radical religious settlement.[2] The Prayer Book, together with Cranmer's Forty-two Articles of Religion, were imposed by a Second Act of Uniformity in 1552. Clerical vestments were forbidden and altars became Communion tables. Attendance at church was enforced by fines and imprisonment for absence. A more violent wave of iconoclasm ensued, including the destruction of statues, paintings, manuscripts and books. The government would not publish Cranmer's revised Canon Law for the church of England because Edward and parliament did not trust episcopal courts to impose discipline effectively. In effect, the church had grown more Calvinistic.[3] Northumberland continued to confiscate the property of Guilds and Chantries and to annex episcopal lands. The founding of the so-called Edwardian grammar schools from the proceeds of monastic spoil were just beginning – their heyday was to be in Elizabeth's reign. This hardly justified the dissolutions, as the 'Demands' of the leaders in the Cornish and East Anglian rebellions made clear.

The rebellions in the years following Henry VIII's death have been described by some historians as 'Mid-Tudor Crisis'.[4] Thomas More's description of government seems apt for these years: 'a conspiracy of rich men procuring their own commodities under the name and title of a commonwealth'.[5]

The attempt to subvert the succession

Under the Henrician settlement, Edward's successor was to be the Princess Mary, the Catholic daughter of Catherine of Aragon. To maintain the Protestant interest and his own, Northumberland thought, at one stage, of by-passing Mary for her 19-year-old half-sister, Elizabeth. Mary, then 36 years old, was the resolute opponent of all that was happening in religion; she would clearly put the clock back on her succession and this would inevitably mark the downfall of all who identified with the Protestant cause; and none was more clearly marked than the duke of Northumberland. To avoid ruin, the duke tried to repeal the Succession Act of 1543 and to alter or set aside the will of Henry VIII. The first would need parliamentary co-operation and also the consent of the young king. Northumberland took much medical advice to assure himself that the young king's illness was terminal; there would certainly be no male heir. Parliament was packed, the council coerced and Edward sufficiently convinced to fall in with Northumberland's designs. He persuaded the dying king to exclude his sister in the name of religion and to settle the succession firstly on the male heirs of Lady Jane Grey whom he had now married to his own son, Guildford Dudley. The 'Device' as it is known, excluded both Mary and Elizabeth, and represented the collateral descendants but only in those of their male heirs. The clear implication was that women were not fit for the throne. Then the original 'Device' was altered by erasure and insertion to read, 'The Lady Jane and her heirs male'.

This brought Lady Jane into the immediate succession to fill the gap between the death of Edward and the birth of a male heir. But, by making this change, Northumberland had virtually signed the death warrant of his son and daughter-in-law. Meanwhile, Princess Mary took refuge on the estates of the duke of Norfolk, ignoring a summons to appear in London at her brother's deathbed. Edward died on 6 July 1553, three months before his sixteenth birthday. Rumours circulated that, in fact, the king had been poisoned. Lady Jane Grey was proclaimed queen in London. Two days later Mary had herself proclaimed the rightful queen of England in Framlingham, in Suffolk; the nation made its choice within the next ten days for Queen Mary as the rightful successor to the Tudor throne. Lady Jane Grey was queen for nine days. In August 1553, Mary and her sister Elizabeth entered London in triumph; Lady Jane and her husband were put in the Tower. Northumberland, already in the Tower, was tried for high treason, condemned and executed on Tower Hill on 22 August 1553.[6]

Northumberland's achievements

Northumberland is usually unfavourably contrasted with Somerset and portrayed as a bad man on the make, causing infinite harm, politically, morally and spiritually. There have been recent attempts to rehabilitate Northumberland by D. Hoak and G. R. Elton. (See the Select bibliography.) But S. T. Bindoff wrote, 'the historian who can praise Somerset's intentions, if not his statesmanship', finds little to relieve the black record of Northumberland's iniquities.[7] And, yet, to redress the balance of judgement: Northumberland abandoned an expensive foreign policy, bringing the French war to an end by surrendering Boulogne. By careful handling of the finances, his Treasurer, the marquis of Winchester, laid the foundations for fiscal reforms, stabilising the currency and prices and thereby curbing inflation. These reforms may eventually have helped Elizabeth to cure this evil at the beginning of her reign.[8] He promoted the Muscovy (Russian) Company of Merchant Adventurers under the expedition sent out under

Sebastian Cabot (who half a century earlier had discovered Newfoundland with his father), Hugh Willoughby and Richard Chancellor, which eventually reached Ivan the Terrible's Moscow. As a result, the trade monopoly in northern Europe of the German Hansa towns was broken.

These seafaring developments belong, however, to a greater age than that of Edward VI. England's last boy-king had been dominated all his life, first by his father and then by his uncles the dukes of Somerset and Northumberland; Edward never had the chance to show his ability to govern. His devotion to Protestantism, his step-mother Catherine Parr, and to his sister Elizabeth come across in his letters. Foreign ambassadors leave no doubt of his intelligent grasp of diplomacy, and his diary recounts his dealings with the Emperor Charles V. In 1552, he drew up a memoranda for parliament in twelve bills for a reorganisation of government suggesting that, had he lived, he might have been an able administrator.

Document case study

Edward VI

5.1 The demands of the Cornish rebels

Six of the sixteen items or articles signed by the chief captains, 1549

1 First we will have the general council and holy decrees of our forefathers observed, kept and performed, and whosoever shall again say them, we hold as Heretics.
2 Item we will have the Laws of our Sovereign Lord King Henry the viii concerning the six articles, to be in use again as in his time they were.
3 Item we will have the mass in Latin, as was before, and celebrated by the Priest without any man or woman communicating with him.
4 Item we will have the Sacrament hang over the High Altar . . .[9]
5 Item we will have the Sacrament of the Altar at Easter delivered to the lay people and then but in one kind.
9 Item we will have every preacher in his sermon and every Priest at his Mass pray specially by name for the souls in purgatory as our forefathers did.

Source: A. Fletcher, *Tudor rebellions*, London, 1968 edn, p. 135

5.2 'Kett's demands being in rebellion', 1549

Six of the twenty-nine items in the above demands signed by Robert Kett, Thomas Cod, Thomas Aldryche and the names of twenty-two representatives of hundreds in Norfolk, Suffolk, and the City of Norwich

1 We pray your Grace that where it is enacted for enclosing that it be not hurtful to such as have enclosed saffren [a plant often used in the manufacture of worsted cloth] grounds for they be greatly chargeable to them.
3 We pray your Grace that no lord of no manor shall come on upon the Commons.
7 We pray that all Bushels within your realm to be of one size, that is to say to be in measure viii gallons.

11 We pray that all freeholders and copyholders may take the profits of all commons and the lords not to take the profits of the same.

16 We pray that all bondsmen be made free for God made all free with his precious bloodshedding.

20 We pray that every parson or vicar having a benefice of £10 or more by year . . . shall teach poor men's children of their parish the book called the catechism and the primer.

Source: A. Fletcher, *Tudor rebellions*, Cambridge, 3rd edn, 1983, pp. 143–44

5.3 The sermon on the ploughers

A sermon preached by Hugh Latimer at St Paul's Cross in 1548

In times past men were full of pity and compassion; but now there is no pity; for in London their brother shall die in the streets for cold; he shall lie sick at the door between stock and stock [between the door posts] and then perish for hunger. In times past when any rich man died in London they were wont to help the scholars at the universities with exhibition. When any man died they would bequeath great sums of money towards the relief of the poor . . . Charity is waxen cold; none helpeth the scholar nor yet the poor; now that the knowledge of God's word is brought to light, and many earnestly study and labour to set it forth now no man almost helpeth to maintain them . . . in the meantime the prelates take their pleasures. They are lords and no labourers; but the devil is diligent at his plough.

Source: Collated from G. E. Corrie, *Sermons by Hugh Latimer*, The Parker Society, Cambridge, 1844

5.4 Edward VII's health

John Banister, physician to King Edward VI, in a medical report of 28 May 1553

In what concerns our king's health be assured of this that he is steadily pining away. He does not sleep except that he be stuffed with drugs . . . but the doctors do not exceed 12 grains at a time . . . and then only if the patient be in great pain or racked by violent coughing . . . the sputum which he brings up is livid, black, fetid and full of carbon; it smells beyond measure . . . his feet are swollen all over . . . to the doctors all these things portend death and that within three months except God of his great mercy spare him.

Source: S. T. Bindoff, 'A kingdom at stake, 1553', in *History today*, September, 1953

5.5 Early Tudor financial policy

Sir Thomas Gresham (1518?–79), was founder of the Royal Exchange, agent of the English crown at Antwerp and the wealthiest London merchant of his time. He was the supposed author of 'Gresham's Law', that 'bad money drives out good'. Here he explains to Mary Tudor how he tried to keep down the rates of exchange on the king's foreign borrowings

. . . in anno 1551 the king's majesty, your late brother, called me to be his agent, and reposed more trust in me as well for the payment of his debts beyond the seas as for the raising of the exchange – being then at 15s and 16s the pound . . . first I practised with the king and my lord Northumberland to overthrow the Steelyard [the London headquarters of the German Hansa merchants] . . . to keep down the exchange . . . Secondly I practised to come in credit with the king's own mere merchants at a set shipping, the exchange still being at 16s that every man should pay the king 15s upon a cloth in Antwerp, to pay at double usance 20s in London which the king's majesty paid them royally . . . which did amount to the sum of £60,000.

Source: J. W. Burgon, 'The life and times of Sir Thomas Gresham', vol. 1, appendix 21, p. 483, from C. H. Williams (ed.), *English historical documents*, vol. 5, London, 1967, p. 1021

Document case-study questions

1 The Western Rebellion of 1549 was motivated by religion. Using 5.1, explain what the rebels were demanding.

2 The Kett Rebellion was motivated by economic concerns. Use 5.2 to explain what those economic concerns were.

3 Documents 5.1 and 5.2 represent a challenge to the authority of the monarchy. In what ways?

4 What is the basis of Latimer's complaints in 5.3? What are the effects of the lack of pity and compassion on mid-Tudor society?

5 Why do you think the health of Edward VI, described in 5.4, was a matter of public concern?

6 What impression of the effectiveness of mid-Tudor financial policy can be found in 5.5?

7 How far do these documents support the assertion that mid-Tudor society was a society in crisis?

Notes and references

1 In the Western church during the Middle Ages, it was normal practice, although both bread and wine were consecrated by the priest during Mass, to distribute Communion to the laity only in one kind or species, in the form of the bread or wafer. At the time of the Reformation, Protestant reformers began to demand that the priest should distribute Communion in both kinds, that is that the congregation should receive both the bread and the wine at Communion. Today, this is practised in both Protestant and Roman Catholic churches.

2 The Mass or Eucharist is the central act of Christian worship. Catholics believe in a 'Real Presence' of Christ's body and blood in an act of 'transubstantiation'. Lutherans also believe in a Real Presence in which Christ's body co-exists with the bread and wine (consubstantiation). The radical Protestant reformers denied any 'Real Presence' at Communion and it is significant that the 1552 Religious Settlement under Northumberland was the only one in England to explicitly deny the Real Presence.

3 John Calvin's reformed church in Geneva became a model for Protestant reformers elsewhere. John Knox in Scotland was one of his most notable followers. Predestination of the elect and salvation by faith alone became central doctrines of Calvinism. The preaching of the Scriptures rather than sacramental rituals was emphasised. Each congregation elected

ministers to preach the Word of God, the Bible. Therefore, in Calvinistic churches, greater prominence was given to the pulpit and a plain table (not an altar) for Communion, which was a commemorative meal of Christ's Last Supper.

4 D. MacCullough, 'Kett's Rebellion in context', *Past and Present*, vol. 84, 1979 and especially D. M. Loades, *The mid-Tudor crisis 1545–1565*, London, 1992. Contemporaries like Sir William Paget saw major challenges to government authority and a radicalism and hostility to the gentry not heard in England since the Peasants' Revolt of 1381.

5 More's classic *Utopia*, while possibly aimed at the early decades of the sixteenth century, has a universal application and can be read with profit for the whole of this theme on Tudor monarchies.

6 Northumberland is buried in St Peter's within the Tower between Anne Boleyn and Catherine Howard and near to the Protector Somerset.

7 S. T. Bindoff, *Tudor England*, London, reprinted 1963.

8 G. R. Elton, *England under the Tudors*, London, 2nd edn, 1974.

9 In pre-Reformation churches in Europe, it was customary to exhibit the Host, or consecrated bread, in a monstrance, a sometimes elaborately decorated vessel or container which was placed above the high altar in a niche. The Host then became an object of devotion to the priest and congregation, especially during the service of Benediction, which was held from time to time. The Reservation of the Sacrament, as it is called, is still practised in the Roman Catholic church and in some Anglican churches today. The practice was bitterly attacked by some Protestant reformers.

6 Mary Tudor: 1553–1558

The accession and early legislation

Northumberland's council, which had proclaimed Lady Jane Grey and denounced Mary Tudor's refusal to submit, ordered the raising of troops, which the duke of Northumberland then led towards Framlingham, in Suffolk, against Mary. A century had passed since the first battle of the Wars of the Roses, and more than half-a-century since the nation saw an armed conflict for the throne. But no battle or war ensued. Mary's support as the rightful queen, daughter of Henry VIII, was total, as Cambridge, East Anglia, London and elsewhere declared for her; the council then proclaimed her and so too did Northumberland as his forces dwindled. Within a week he was in the Tower with his son and daughter-in-law.

Mary soon removed from office most of Northumberland's supporters and promoted those loyal to her and her faith. Bishop Stephen Gardiner, for example, who had been imprisoned under Edward VI, was released from the Tower to become Lord Chancellor. Other conservative bishops were also set free; but firm religious lines were not at first drawn in England, any more than they were in France or Germany. Ten of Edward's bishops continued in office as did many parish clergy; those who lost office did so for being married and not for dogmatic reasons. In fact, those elements of English society which had benefited from the Henrician and Edwardian Reformations seemed determined to keep all the independence that they had won for church and state, as well as any church properties they had gained from the dissolutions.

However, S. T. Bindoff points out how religious changes were at first 'left incline and then right about turn'; for, within six months of her accession, England was again a Catholic kingdom. Two personal decisions of Mary would consolidate and confirm her opposition to English Protestantism; her decision to marry Philip of Spain and the revival of the statutes against heresy, especially *de heretico comburendo*, in 1555, which provided for the burning of heretics and earned her the nickname of 'Bloody Mary'. This act restored to the ecclesiastical courts the powers to deal with heresy which Henry VIII had taken from them; here lay the origin of the Marian persecution of Protestants.

Some historians see in both decisions that Mary had cut herself off from her subjects' growing sense of national and Protestant identity. After all, the English nation had accepted five distinct changes in their religion in thirty years without any great turmoil and, had Mary stopped when she restored matters as they were at the death of her father, all may have been well. Allegiance to the papacy ran counter to nationalistic feelings. Moreover, when Mary married into the Spanish royal family, and lost Calais, the last English possession on the continent, she forfeited the earlier support and affection of her people.

From Mary's point of view, however, nothing was more natural for her, with her Catholic upbringing, than to lean towards Spain, the home of her slighted mother and of the emperor, her only friend when Englishmen had forsaken her. If Mary were to undo the Reformation she needed an heir, otherwise the crown and the religious destiny of England would pass to the Princess Elizabeth whose very birth caused the breach with Rome, and whose right to succeed to the throne depended on the rejection of papal authority. There was still, however, a deep prejudice against women rulers and when a queen regnant decided to take a consort, it also meant conferring the kingdom upon a foreign equal. This could jeopardise national independence. This was Mary Tudor's dilemma. When she finally made her decision for the Habsburg match with Philip, it was made against the advice of her council, and her parliament, and this brought out the full hostility of the English populace against all foreigners which was then rampant.

Three main problems, therefore, confronted Mary: the punishment of traitors, the religious settlement, and the question of her marriage. In all of them, she was advised by the emperor's resident ambassador, Simon Renard. England under Mary, however, was never a pawn of the emperor's and Renard often found Mary Tudor less than amenable to his advice against the proposed marriage to Charles's recently widowed son Philip. He was twenty-six, about eleven years younger than Mary, although the age difference may not have been Renard's chief objection to the proposed marriage.

Both Charles and Renard urged her to be ruthless in the punishment of traitors, but they tried to restrain her religious enthusiasm and persuade her to act cautiously in the restoration of Catholicism and in the persecution of Protestants. Her dislike of sex made Mary reluctant to marry; many historians assert that her high principles and lack of any kind of vindictiveness made her innocent of the necessary political duplicity to use trumped up charges for executing her political opponents. Their view is that it was her forthright and eager religious temperament and convictions that made her want to stamp out heresy.

Renard advised Mary to execute Jane Grey, her husband Dudley, the earls of Suffolk and Northumberland and any lords of the council who had supported Jane. He, moreover, advised that her half-sister Elizabeth should be arrested as she was a potential focus for Protestant rivals and rebels. Mary would not agree to these proposals, at first claiming, for example, that Jane Grey was an innocent dupe and that she would not have her sister imprisoned. In August 1553, she agreed to the execution of Northumberland and his two main agents, Palmer and Gates, who were sent to the block on 22 August.[1] Mary ordered that wide publicity be given to Northumberland's recantation of Protestantism.

The religious settlement

By Henry VIII's Act of Supremacy, the sovereign was Supreme Head of the church. This title was irksome to Mary, but it did not stop her using its power to restore Catholicism, before divesting herself of it and handing it back to the pope. The emperor advised her not to do anything about religion until she had eliminated her political rivals. Mary refused to abide by this advice. She was determined to make England Catholic straightaway.[2]

On the delicate question of parliamentary powers in matters of religion, Mary had a different approach. The Reformation statutes came to be regarded as binding in law in all circumstances until repealed by parliament, certainly this was the case under Henry VIII. But Mary would not permit Protestant acts of parliament to be enforced against Catholics, even though they had not yet been repealed. Like Sir Thomas More, Mary did not recognise an act of parliament as absolute in all circumstances; in fact, both regarded a parliamentary statute as null and void if it was in conflict with the universal and fundamental law of Christendom. Those who put all their trust in the sovereignty of parliament, like Sir James Hales in both Edward's and Mary's reigns, clashed with both sovereigns. For example, as a judge of the assize Hales went about enforcing the Act of Uniformity in Maidstone, Kent, against Catholics who attended Mass. The queen ordered him to stop his convictions and he took his stand on the fact that the Act of Uniformity had not been repealed by parliament, and the command of the queen could not alter the law of the land.[3]

Mary was greatly encouraged in restoring Catholicism by clerical support in Convocation and by the conversion of former Protestants. Mary was popular in that she also refused to collect taxes voted by Northumberland in the last parliament of Edward VI and in her expulsion of French, Dutch and Flemish Protestant refugees from England. Some theologians, however, stayed with Cranmer at Lambeth Palace. Many of those expelled were the emperor's subjects, and suffered arrest and persecution when they landed in Antwerp.

Married clergy were ordered to put away their wives in the spring of 1554. Many of them were deprived of their benefices, about 20 per cent in the dioceses of south-eastern England, but likely as high as a third in London, Essex and Norfolk. Popular Protestantism had made little progress north of the Trent. Mary's parliament of October 1553 passed acts annulling the divorce of Henry VIII and Catherine of Aragon, thereby legitimising the queen herself. Another act restored the Mass throughout England as from 21 December, suppressed the Book of Common Prayer and made it illegal to attend Protestant services.

The Spanish marriage

Tudors and Habsburgs had long been allies, especially as the Netherlands and the cloth market at Antwerp had been the staple of English commerce. In the tortuous arrangements for the future marriage of Mary to Philip of Spain,

Stephen Gardiner, skilled lawyer and trusted bishop of Winchester, ensured all kinds of guarantees in the marriage treaty. All state documents, for example, were to be issued in the name of 'Mary and Philip, queen and king of England' and 'both such be advised in all matters relating to England by English ministers only'; nor should England be required to declare war on France (the emperor was constantly at war with France). In the financial arrangements for the dowry, Mary had by far the best of the bargain. Counts Egmont and Lalaing were sent to finalise the marriage negotiations but, as soon as the news of the marriage spread throughout the land, hostile demonstrations took place especially in London and the south. Even while negotiations were going on, the council was arresting potential rebels. Within a couple of weeks of the marriage contract being signed, Queen Mary faced perhaps the greatest threat of her reign in the rebellion of Sir Thomas Wyatt.[4]

The Wyatt Rebellion

Wyatt planned the rising for January 1554, just before the arrival of Philip in England. The success of the conspiracy depended on secrecy and the enthusiasm of the local gentry for a political cause, because there was no economic crisis. Wild rumours of Spanish intentions fanned the latent hostility of ordinary English folk against foreigners. Sir James Croft, who had been Lord Deputy of Ireland from 1551 to 1552, Sir Peter Carew, who helped to put down the Western Rebellion in 1549, and Sir Thomas Wyatt of the Kentish gentry were the leaders; they were motivated by a mixture of self-interest, for they depended on court patronage for offices and advancement, and national pride or idealism.

Wyatt raised 3,000 men to march on London. Simultaneous risings in Devon, the Midlands and Wales collapsed, however, due to the government's fore-knowledge. The French were to supply naval support in the Channel to secure the south-western ports against any possible Spanish landings. Wyatt was to contain the south-east against attack from the Netherlands – it always sounded a note of dire warning to the crown if the powerful Kentish gentry came to head a rebellion. The conspirators may have aimed to persuade Elizabeth to marry Edward Courtenay, a great grandson of Edward IV and to depose Queen Mary in her favour. Wyatt had put out much propaganda and had sufficient strength to march on London, first to Blackheath, and then advance to Southwark without much opposition. He demanded the custody of the Tower and the queen as a hostage. Mary appealed to the Londoners' loyalty and they rose to the occasion. In her speech to them at the Guildhall she reminded them that Wyatt and his companions were 'rank traitors'; the question of her marriage was 'but a Spanish cloak to cover their pretended purpose against our religion'; and in any case she would abide by parliament's advice on the marriage. Her appeal to their hearts then displayed the skill in flattery of the Tudors: 'Certainly if a prince and governor may as naturally and earnestly love her subjects as the mother doth love the child, then assure yourselves that I, being your lady and mistress do as earnestly and tenderly love and favour you.'[5]

Wyatt soon found that London Bridge was manned by forces loyal to the queen. He then marched to cross the Thames at Kingston, intending to advance on the City from the west, but at Hyde Park, about three kilometres from the walls of the city, his way forward was blocked; desultory fighting took place up as far as Ludgate Hill. Many deserted Wyatt, and his attenuated army of rebels was hemmed in and overwhelmed. With his surrender, the rebellion collapsed. Had Mary taken Gardiner's advice to flee the city, she may have lost both London and the kingdom. Wyatt and his chief men were taken to the Tower and his men herded into the prisons and city churches.

Mary's attitude to her political opponents now changed; she was ready to act on Renard's advice to use expediency rather than justice. A week after the ending of the rebellion, Lady Jane Grey and her husband were convicted of high treason and beheaded on 12 February. Both were victims of another's recklessness and innocent of any part in Wyatt's rising. They were followed to the block by her father, the duke of Suffolk, who had tried to raise the Midlands for Wyatt, by her uncle Thomas Grey and by Wyatt himself on 11 April. About a hundred of his rank and file were hanged. On 18 March, Elizabeth was sent to the Tower. Although Renard could not persuade Mary to have Elizabeth executed, the queen ordered the heir to the throne to be arrested on a charge of high treason. Elizabeth had passionately denied all disloyal complicity with either Courtenay or Wyatt, who insisted, even on the scaffold, that Elizabeth was innocent. After two months in the Tower, Elizabeth was sent to her house at Woodstock where she waited the turn of fortune. Courtenay was also released and allowed to go to Italy where he died.

The punishing of traitors and potential political opponents was the major result of Wyatt's rising. Politics and religion were, however, inextricably linked, and it was soon the turn of the major heretics to suffer at the hands of Mary, in her desire to return England to an uncompromising Catholicism.

The Catholic restoration

The new king was a foreigner; but the new papal legate, Cardinal Reginald Pole, was a descendant of English kings, and related to Mary.[6] Staunch loyalty to Rome brought his mother and brother to the block but he escaped with a 20-year exile from England. The emperor would not allow his return until Philip was well established. The Lords and Commons had to repeal his act of attainder to make his reception into the country legal.

The repeal of the Act of Supremacy

On 29 November 1554, parliament repealed the Henrician Act of Supremacy; unanimously, in the Lords, but with only two dissenting votes in the Commons. The ease with which this legislation was passed was mainly because a papal dispensation had been gained for those who had church lands and properties allowing them to be retained. Land and property was just as important to the members of these Marian parliaments as religion. The queen went out of her way to restore lands that remained with the crown. She was unable to persuade her landed subjects to do the same. A contemporary Venetian ambassador is supposed to have reported: 'The English in general would turn Jews or Turks if their sovereign pleased but not at the price of the monastic lands.' However, with the realm re-united to Rome and the Heresy Act on the Statute Book, all Mary needed was an heir, who would be brought up as a Catholic so that Elizabeth would be excluded and Catholicism preserved.

The Marian martyrs

Against the advice of the emperor and Philip, the trials and burnings of heretics went forward in February 1555. The first Protestant martyr was John Rogers, burnt at Smithfield on 4 February. Some 300 people suffered this dreadfully brutal death. A third were clergy, and among the lay victims were 60 women. More than two-thirds of the Protestant martyrs came from London and the six home counties; there was only one burning north of Chester; many in Norfolk, Suffolk, and Sussex and several in the Midlands, Gloucestershire and South Wales. The victims came from all classes of society except the nobility; apart from the five bishops, Cranmer, Ridley, Latimer, Hooper and Ferrar, who had been the leading theologians under Edward VI, there were country gentlemen, merchants from the boroughs, artisans and labouring men and women. Nor did they all hold the same views. In fact, some held such extreme views that they might well have been burned as heretics by the same Protestant bishops who were their fellow martyrs. One, for example, denied the divinity of Christ. By the standards of Europe's religious wars, the number of English martyrs was small; nevertheless the Marian persecution, unique in English history, did much harm to the Catholic cause in which Mary believed. For four centuries, Catholics suffered some degree of persecution and victimisation because of what happened in England under Mary between 1555 and 1558. John Foxe's celebrated *Book of martyrs*, with its vivid woodcuts, became at once a memorial, a reminder and an inspiration to Protestant England under Elizabeth. She ordered a copy to be set up in every church and it became the most widely read and possessed of English classics.[7] The Marian persecution became firmly connected in the folk memory with the rule of a Spanish king and the supremacy of an Italian pope. S. T. Bindoff's judgement is particularly perceptive on this aspect of the reign: 'During her brief reign Mary Tudor was her church's greatest asset in England; since the day of her death her memory has always been its greatest liability.'[8]

Mary's last years

Despite safeguards in the Spanish marriage, England was inevitably brought into the Habsburg sphere of influence and against its enemy France. In the war between the emperor and France, Calais fell without resistance. This was considered a national disgrace and bit deeply into the hearts of both queen and people. During the 18 months that Philip spent in England, hopes of a child and a Catholic succession faded. Philip retired to the Netherlands. Mary fell seriously ill in the spring of 1558; discontent and disillusion surrounded her final year. The

The family of Henry VIII: an allegory of the Tudor succession, painted by Lucas de Heere (1534–84) around 1570–75 (panel). King Henry is shown with Edward VI kneeling by his left side. Elizabeth stands in a prominent position on the right of the picture followed by the goddess Flora and the fruits of peace. Mary and her husband Philip II stand on the left, followed by Mars the god of war. What events justified the artist's interpretations of the reigns of Mary and Elizabeth?

new pope, Paul IV, became pro-French and anti-Habsburg. Gardiner, her ablest minister, was dead. Pole was disappointed at not gaining the papacy. Her council was torn apart with faction and, in the nation at large, her policy of suppressing heresy had not been successful. Protestant prayer meetings and heretical and seditious books were circulating in London. On 17 November 1558 – a day celebrated by English Protestants for more than a century as Queen Elizabeth's Accession Day – Mary died. Some hours later in Lambeth Palace, Cardinal Pole followed her. She was given a full Catholic funeral in Westminster Abbey; John White, Gardiner's successor at Winchester, preached the eulogy and, because at one stage his sermon proved critical of Elizabeth, he was firmly placed under house arrest. In her will, Mary wanted her mother's body brought from Peterborough Cathedral and buried beside her in Westminster Abbey, but Elizabeth found it politically inexpedient to put Mary's will into effect.

Finally, the reaction to persecution and foreign rule was skilfully exploited, not least by John Foxe and other exiled propagandists. In this way, a very powerful myth of popular and Protestant patriotism was created which influenced political consciousness for centuries after Mary's death.

Document case study

Mary Tudor

6.1 Some early legislation

'An act for the repeal of certain statutes . . . of Edward VI'

Be it enacted that . . . the Act for the receiving of the Sacrament of the Altar in both kinds . . . and also one for the election of Bishops . . . another entitled An Act for the Uniformity of Service and Administration of the Sacraments throughout the realm . . . another entitled An Act to take away all positive laws made against the marriage of priests . . . and an Act for the abolishing and putting away of divers books, and images . . . also an Act for the Uniformity of Common Prayer . . . an Act made for the marriage of priests and the legitimation of their children . . . every clause, sentence, branch, article mentioned, expressed or contained in the said statutes shall be henceforth utterly repelled, void, annihilate and of none effect.

Source: *The statutes of the realm*, vol. 4, 202, from I Mary 2, c. 2, 1553, HMSO, 1810–1828

6.2 The opinion of Bishop Gardiner, the Chancellor, on the position of the papal legate, Cardinal Pole

Extract from the Spanish ambassador's report in England to the Emperor Charles V, 8 August 1554

Sire, we have talked over with the Chancellor [Stephen Gardiner] and the Bishop of Ely, Cardinal Pole's demand to come over here at once as Papal Legate and set about the execution of his commission to establish once more the authority of the holy see and put an end to religious disputes . . . The Chancellor's view might be represented as that of his coming to take possession – of the archbishopric of Canterbury, to which he has been appointed, to congratulate their Highnesses on their marriage, or to take up the thread of his former endeavour to get the Queen to intervene in the cause of peace . . . he thinks neither the Council nor Parliament be allowed to dictate in this matter for they would never consent to his coming at all . . . Above all before coming to England he must clear up this business of the tenure of holders of Church property in such a manner that the present possessors may be convinced that they will not be disturbed.

Source: R. Tyler (ed.), *Calendar of state papers, Spanish*, vol. 13, 1554–58, vols. 10–13, HMSO, 1954, pp. 22–23

6.3 Queen Mary's Guildhall speech

From a speech made to the Londoners and recorded by John Foxe, her implacable enemy

I am your Queen, she said, to whom at my coronation when I was wedded to the realm and laws of the same (the spousal ring whereof I have on my finger, which never hereto was, nor hereafter shall be, left off) you promised your allegiance and obedience unto me . . . And I say to you, on the word of a Prince, I cannot tell how naturally the mother loveth the child, for I was never the mother of any; but certainly if a Prince and Governor may as naturally and earnestly love her subjects as the mother doth love the child, then assure yourselves that I, being your lady and mistress, do as earnestly and tenderly love and favour you. And I thus loving you, cannot but think that ye as heartily and faithfully love me; and then I doubt not but we shall give these rebels a short and speedy overthrow.

Source: Jasper Ridley, *Mary Tudor*, London, 1973, p. 146

6.4 Wyatt's Rebellion

From 'The chronicle of Queen Jane', a pocket diary kept by an officer in the royal service in the Tower of London, c. 1554

[a] This day Sir Nicholas Poynes . . . being an assistant at the Tower, was with the queen to know whether they shoot off at the Kentishmen (with cannon), and so beat down the houses upon their heads. 'Nay', said the queen, 'that were pity, for many poor men and householders are like to be undone there and killed. For, saith she, 'I trust, God willing, that they shall be fought with tomorrow.'

[b] This said Wyatt, with his men, marched still forward all along to Temple Bar, also through Fleet Street along till he came to Ludgate his men going not in any good order or array. It is said in Fleet Street certain of the Lord Treasurer's band, to the number of three hundred men met them and so going on the one side passed by them coming on the other side without any whit saying to them. Also this is more strange . . . Wyatt and his company passed along by a great company of harassed men . . . most with their swords drawn, some cried 'Queen Mary hath granted our request, and given us pardon.'

[c] On Ash Wednesday that Wyatt was at Charing Cross did Doctor Weston, priest, sing Mass before the Queen in harness under his vestments.

Source: J. G. Nichols, *The chronicle of Queen Jane and two years of Queen Mary* (ed. from B. M. Harleian MS 194), Camden Society, vol. 48, London, 1850

6.5 The Spanish ambassador on the dangers of Marian persecution

Simon Renard to Philip II of Spain, 5 February 1555 (letter)

Sire: the people of this town of London are murmuring about the cruel enforcement of the recent acts of parliament on heresy which has now begun, as shown publicly when a certain Rogers was burnt yesterday. Some of the onlookers wept others prayed to God to give them strength . . . others gathered the ashes and bones . . . yet others threatening the bishops. The haste with which the bishops have proceeded in this matter may well cause a revolt . . . I do not think it well that your Majesty should allow further executions to take place unless the reasons are overwhelmingly strong . . . tell the bishops that they are not to proceed to such lengths without having first consulted you and the Queen . . . Your Majesty will also consider that the Lady Elizabeth has her supporters and that there are Englishmen who do not love foreigners.

Source: R. Tyler (ed.), *Calendar of state papers, Spanish*, vol. 13, 1554–58, HMSO, 1954, p. 138

Document case-study questions

1 What did 6.1 seek to repeal? Why did Mary wish to repeal legislation passed by her brother?

2 Document 6.2 identifies several problems Mary faced in returning England to Catholicism. What were they and why were they problems?

3 What message is Mary giving to the Londoners in 6.3?

4 How far does the fact that her enemy, John Foxe, recorded the speech affect its reliability to the historian?

5 What information can be gained from 6.4 about Wyatt's Rebellion and Mary's attitudes to her people?

6 Document 6.5 is a Spanish source. What concerns does it express and how accurate do you think those concerns were?

7 In 1553 Mary was welcomed as monarch. By 1555 her reign was effectively in ruins. How far do these documents help explain this viewpoint?

Notes and references

1 Northumberland recanted before his death, converting to Catholicism and stating that it was Protestantism which led him into treason. Years later Protestant propagandists turned his arguments to their advantage arguing how Northumberland who had ruled corruptly and had committed treason against Queen Mary had always been a Catholic.

2 For example, instead of attending the funeral service of her brother Edward conducted according to the Book of Common Prayer, Queen Mary attended a private Mass in the Tower.

3 Hales was dismissed from office as a judge, arrested and imprisoned in the King's Bench prison; he was released after a year, but committed suicide.

4 A month after Wyatt's Rebellion, Mary was married by proxy to Philip in Whitehall. Five months later, in July 1554, Philip landed at Southampton. Mary met him at Winchester where in Gardiner's cathedral they were solemnly married on 25 July, St James' Day, 1554.

5 Cited in A. Fletcher, *Tudor rebellions*, Harlow, 3rd edn, 1983.

6 His mother, the countess of Salisbury, was the daughter of the duke of Clarence, brother of King Edward IV.

7 Foxe, a Lincolnshire vicar, had already written on Protestant martyrs who had suffered for their faith from the time of the Lollards to the death of Henry VIII. To this, he added an account of the early Christian martyrs under the Caesars, to associate them with the martyrs of his own times. On Mary's accession, he went abroad with his book and completed it with accounts of the Marian martyrs.

8 S. T. Bindoff, *Tudor England*, London, 1963 edn, p. 179.

7 Elizabeth I: the early years, 1558–1588

An insecure accession

Elizabeth was 25 years old at her accession to the throne of England on 17 November 1558. All her life she had experienced the perils of proximity to the throne, treading cautiously among Catholics and Protestants and among those who wished to use her as a pawn in the power game. No doubt she reflected on the errors made by her predecessors and planned not to repeat them; her father gambled all for an heir, her brother became the instrument of jealous factions and her sister made a disastrous foreign marriage and became fanatical in returning the realm to Roman Catholicism. Her experience of rebellions in her predecessors' time had taught Elizabeth the virtues of discretion. When the Spanish ambassador boldly suggested to Elizabeth that she owed her survival and present prospects as queen to Philip, her Spanish brother-in-law, she replied that the people of England had placed her where she was. There was no machinery to discover the will of the people nor had the 'people' ever been consulted about a royal accession, but Elizabeth sincerely believed that the monarchy had its foundation in the English nation. She, therefore, would place no reliance on foreign princes, their promises or their military and naval forces.

To the new queen, the main danger areas were religion, faction and the question of the succession. If the religious settlement leaned too far to Protestantism, her Catholic subjects would be alienated and vice versa. If she named a Protestant heir, all Catholic Europe would be up in arms against her and, if she named a Catholic one, her establishment of the Anglican church would come to nothing. In either case, the result would mean the growth of factions. Her political acumen in keeping all decisions on religion and the succession as a prerogative of the crown, as well as her longevity and general good health,[1] may very well have made the celebrated Elizabethan Age possible. After decades of putting off suitors, it became clear that she would not have a child of her own to succeed. Any foreign match would have brought the nation directly into the European power-struggle. On the other hand, marriage with an English nobleman would have allied the queen with a politico-religious faction. Only when the Scottish and Spanish threats had disappeared, did Elizabeth name James of Scotland her heir.

Throughout her long reign, Elizabeth maintained a precarious political and religious balance when England needed stability. In S. T. Bindoff's judgement, her fame may be said to have rested on 'her longevity, her long-preserved virginity, and her political genius'.[2] All her biographers have remarked upon her quick intelligence, her deviousness and calculating spirit, her gift for choosing able ministers, her ability to dissemble and compromise. There could be no doubt who her father was. It was a gift of fortune that she reigned for 45 years and, in much of that time, she depended on the hard work and total loyalty of an able minister, William Cecil, later Lord Burghley. He was a survivor, having conformed to the state religion of three reigns, though his family relationships and leanings were Protestant. Above all, however, he was a shrewd steward of the national economy and the state treasury. In that, he was at one with the queen, who had inherited her grandfather's parsimony and, likely, his scepticism. On Cecil's appointment as chief minister, Elizabeth said, 'This judgement I have of you that you will not be corrupted with any manner of gifts, and that you will be faithful to the state.' Her choice of privy councillors was also indicative of future Elizabethan politics; there were seven new members but eleven had served under Mary, who tended to appoint churchmen; eventually Elizabeth's privy council would be an exclusively lay body. Religion, however, proved to be the most pressing problem.

The problem of religion

There had been a swing to Protestantism under Edward and, under Mary, the pendulum had swung equally back to Catholicism. More than likely, the Protestant exiles from the Marian persecution and the fires of Smithfield, not to speak of the loss of Calais, had kept the embers of Protestantism glowing in the last years of Mary's reign. Moreover, Cardinal Pole and his colleagues on the episcopal bench had not done much to promote the zeal of the Counter or Catholic Reformation which was renewing continental Catholicism, especially from the Jesuit-run seminaries.

England, and much of Europe, waited for Elizabeth to settle religion; a change was expected, but the details would have to wait on parliament. Clearly, the English Protestant community expected a return to some form of Protestant settlement; to them, Elizabeth was the English Deborah sent to deliver and save God's Englishmen as the Deborah of the Old Testament had saved the Israelites. Despite her conformity to Catholic practice in her sister's reign, Elizabeth was a convinced moderate Protestant, whose religious beliefs rested on her religious and humanistic education, rather than on evangelical conversion. Furthermore, the authority of the ruler in spiritual matters won by her father was not to be thrown away; to Elizabeth, her sister Mary had no power to abandon the title of Supreme Head; in her eyes the title was inherent in the nature of kingship. And, in this concept of the royal government of the church and state, it followed that the sovereign should legislate for a uniform mode of public worship. The subject would be required to attend the form of worship authorised by the state as a public duty, rather than out of doctrinal orthodoxy. It was practical and political considerations, enforced by her advisers like William Cecil and Matthew Parker,[3] that made Elizabeth opt for a moderate Protestant settlement. It, in turn, offered greater advantages than a continuation of the Catholic restoration, which would have brought with it with the real danger of Mary Stuart's succession. Many historians have speculated on Elizabeth's choice between Catholicism and the Protestant creed for which Cranmer and Ridley died. Why, in fact, did she choose the Protestant path? On the other hand, what were the advantages for Elizabeth in keeping England Catholic?

Cecil and the queen worked so closely that it is difficult to distinguish which policies or aspects of policy were Elizabeth's and which Cecil's. Pliant advisers in the council urged that the new settlement of religion must be the last. In a sense it was, for it is clear that, despite confusion amongst her subjects, inertia among the majority and theological controversy among the minority, the Elizabethan ecclesiastical settlement and system laid the foundations of later Anglicanism. Richard Hooker (1553–1600) in his *Laws of ecclesiastical polity* would give the Anglican church a definitive statement of doctrine.[4]

The Elizabethan settlement

The settlement of religion was thrashed out in the queen's first parliament, which sat from January to April 1559. The royal supremacy was re-enacted and gave the queen the same ecclesiastical authority as her father, but under the title of 'Supreme Governor'. The act abolished papal power once again. In the Lords, and in the meetings of the two Convocations of Canterbury and York, the bishops resisted, but the remaining stubborn Marian bishops were deprived of their bishoprics, and replaced by a new bench of bishops led by Matthew Parker. The clerical rank and file, less heroic, took the line of least resistance. Elizabeth wanted the restoration of the 1549 Prayer Book, which she thought acceptable to both the Protestant party and to the majority who were largely unaffected by the Counter or Catholic Reformation. However, the 1559 Act of Uniformity restored the second Edwardian Prayer Book of 1552 as the legal form for the services. By a deliberate vagueness on matters of minor controversy, it was capable of either a Catholic or a Protestant interpretation. There was, therefore, a compromise on the question of the Real Presence; the 1552 Prayer Book which implied that Communion was a symbolic commemorative act was supplemented by words from the 1549 Book which suggested Christ's Body was really present in the Eucharist. Refusals to attend the church's services became punishable by a fine.[5] (See p. 77.) Royal injunctions to Protestantise the church, and to enforce the Book of Common Prayer, as well as the use of the Edwardian vestments and the ornaments of the churches, were published, and all were to be implemented by visitations of the queen's commissioners. Therefore, in the Supremacy Oath and in her ecclesiastical commissions, such as the Courts of High Commission of Canterbury and York, the queen had her powers fully defined. In them, she had weapons enough to impose her will on any opposition. The simple administration of the oath made it easy to remove obstructive clergy without raising difficult questions of doctrine. It was simply presented as a matter of loyalty to the sovereign. In the visitations that followed, some 300 clergy were deprived of their livings. In 1563, Convocation adopted a revised version of Cranmer's Forty-Two Articles, the Thirty-Nine Articles. These avoided a direct attack on Catholic belief, but Article 17 sanctioned a belief in the Calvinistic doctrine of Predestination, and affirmed the church's right to regulate rites and ceremonial. The structure was now complete. The settlement found favour with the majority of the people, even though all but one of the bishops refused to take the Oath of Supremacy and were consequently deprived of their sees. Probably about one-third of the parish clergy were likewise deprived of their livings. The importance of the Elizabethan church settlement lies in the fact that the church was now a state church under the domination of the crown. Therefore, religious opposition to the settlement would be considered to be political opposition to the state. Opposition would come from many Roman Catholics and from the puritans – the extreme Protestants who were dissatisfied with the settlement. Catholicism would emerge as both an internal and external threat.[6]

Incidentally, the peace made with France at the Treaty of Cateau-Cambrésis in April 1559 had no influence on the making of the church settlement, nor did it have any impact on relations with Spain. This is because Philip was then protecting Elizabeth's interests at the papal court and even exploring the possibility of a Habsburg marriage alliance with the queen.

Puritan opposition

In the early days of the settlement, a 'puritan' was one who wanted further reform of doctrine from within the church, structural changes in its organisation, and changes in its ceremonies and practices. Elizabethan puritans, at that time, ranged from extremists like the Cambridge theologian, Thomas Cartwright, and the MP, Peter Wentworth, who both wanted a complete change in the system of church organisation, from an episcopal system of government to a Presbyterian one, to moderates like Cecil, the earl of Leicester and Archbishop Parker. These moderates, who were closely associated with the queen, were content with reforms on points of ritual such as the abolition of the ring in marriage and the sign of the cross at baptism. But many influential puritans, like Wentworth, were in the House of Commons when, as early as the first Elizabethan parliament, it objected to the adoption of the 1549 Prayer Book.[7]

With a growing stream of graduate clerics from the universities being appointed to vacant livings, the puritan 'movement' began to spread. After 1570, the movement began to take on a Presbyterian complexion, so that by 1580 a system of 'classes' had been set up in various shires. These were semi-Presbyterian meetings or cells, composed of all sympathetic clergy in a particular area who were trying to adapt the services and organisation of the Established church to a more Presbyterian model. This involved mutual instruction and correction of faults with a fellowship of ministers. In the Presbyterian model, parish congregations each 'elected' their own minister and were supervised by a consistory made up of elders from a group of parishes. The system of classes was a radical challenge to the royal supremacy.

In parliament, the London puritan clerics, John Field and Thomas Wilcox, circulated their *Admonition to parliament* in an attempt to reform the church through parliament rather than through the queen or the bishops. Both were imprisoned in Newgate in 1572, and the scourge of puritans, the future Archbishop Whitgift, composed replies to the *Admonition*. However, a counter-reply came in the circulation of the *Second admonition*, calling for a Presbyterian system of church government. As Thomas Cartwright escaped abroad at this time, it is likely he was its author.[8]

The essential issue for the puritans in their quarrel with those who supported the Elizabethan church settlement, to which all else took second place, was that religion should serve the greater glory of God and man's salvation through the application of one rule only, the rule of Holy Scripture. To men like Cartwright, the Bible could not justify the episcopal system of church government. It seemed to the puritans that the Established church was more concerned with supporting the kingdom of England than the kingdom of God.

In the late 1580s, the puritans launched a particularly radical propaganda campaign in the anonymous Martin Marprelate Tracts – a series of seven scurrilously satirical attacks on the church and individual bishops. Government spies sought out the underground presses and, in so doing, exposed a whole puritan network which had, to a great extent, escaped Archbishop Whitgift's use of the Court of High Commission. This court was an instrument he had used with considerable success to discipline the church since his consecration as archbishop in 1583. But, intent on repressing non-conformity, Whitgift did not wish to make puritan martyrs as Queen Mary had created Protestant ones. In his Articles of 1585, moreover, he set about reforming genuine grievances in the church, but he was an administrator rather than a theologian and was, therefore, more concerned about discipline than dogma. Between 1589 and 1593 at least four puritan radicals or separatists were executed and many others banished. Under an active and determined Whitgift, the full panoply of the church courts was brought to bear on puritan dissent so that it lost most of its vigour and many ardent puritans reluctantly conformed in the final decade of the reign. Uniformity, the keystone of the system, was never utterly complete, secret celebrations of the Mass went on in the manor houses of the older gentry among whom a coherent, organised Catholic community existed – an underground church as it were – and to which many government officials turned a blind eye.

The Catholic threat

English Catholics were remarkably quiet in the first decade of the reign; to a great extent the Catholic laity under Mary became Anglican under Elizabeth. Catholics enjoyed a large measure of toleration in these first years of the reign and although, in the church's eyes, Elizabeth was ineligible to be queen because of her illegitimacy, neither of the contemporary popes, Paul IV and Pius IV, contested her title. Elizabeth was not excommunicated until 1570. Furthermore, the Catholic powers, France and Spain, sought Elizabeth's friendship. In fact,

Philip II proposed marriage to her. All of this was a far cry from raising a European Catholic league against the heretical queen of England. In England, her government was content in the early years with a minimum standard of outward conformity and did not unduly disturb the north and west of the country, where the Mass and the practice of the old faith had not died out. The situation then changed dramatically in 1568, when Catholicism became a major threat.

In that year, William Allen founded a missionary college at Douai, in Flanders, specifically to train priests to reconvert England to Roman Catholicism. Allen was determined not to wait for better times but to make them better. Douai became the centre for ardent English Catholics with a passionate mission to bring England back to Catholicism. In 1568, too, Philip II had sent the duke of Alva into the Netherlands to crush a rebellion against the Spaniards. Consequently, the prospect of a Spanish military power just across the Channel confronted Elizabeth; her ministers convinced her that it was her duty to frustrate Philip's plans in the Netherlands, a policy which eventually would mean war with Spain.

Spain, the leading Catholic power and promoter of the Counter Reformation in Europe, now clearly became a threat to England. Philip's agents helped and encouraged English Catholic exiles to rise against Elizabeth in the series of plots then being hatched in Spain, the Netherlands and at Rome.

In 1568, the arrival of the fugitive Mary Queen of Scots in England presented Elizabeth with grave problems. In the eyes of many Catholics, Mary was already the rightful queen of England, and if Elizabeth should die she had a powerful claim to the succession. Until the day of her execution in 1587, Mary Queen of Scots became the focus of conspiratorial plots against Elizabeth engineered by English Catholics, Spanish agents and the political opponents of the queen and Cecil. These especially included those at court in the anti-Cecil faction and, above all, the Catholic earls of the North, such as Thomas Percy, seventh earl of Northumberland.

The Northern Rebellion, 1569

The causes of the rebellion

Mary's future became the catalyst of court politics, for example plans were laid to marry the Scottish queen to the premier duke of England, the duke of Norfolk. This made him the focus of a conspiracy that attracted a substantial part of the nobility. Indeed, leading Protestants like the earl of Leicester and the English ambassador in Paris, Sir Nicholas Throckmorton, saw in the marriage a good solution to the two major problems; what to do with Mary Queen of Scots and how to settle the succession question. By means of the Norfolk marriage to Mary, the queen could then make a lasting peace with both France and Spain and settle her succession into the bargain. And, from the point of view of their political ambitions, it could lead to the overthrow of Cecil at court. But Elizabeth would have none of it when the plans became known. Leicester was cashiered for his attack on Cecil, and Norfolk left the court under a cloud for his home at Kenninghall in Norfolk, refusing a summons to the queen at Windsor. A rebellion was expected, but Norfolk was indecisive. Northumberland was ready to raise his tenantry in support of a Catholic rising but in his own words 'not to hazard myself for the marriage'; he was a reluctant recruit to the marriage plot and his local grievances against crown exactions had more in common with those of Neville, earl of Westmorland, and Lord Dacre. The three were the linchpins of the rebellion, and tenant loyalty and that of their retainers explains the support they had.

The earls issued a proclamation for the rebellion which consistently stressed that the official reason for the uprising was to resist the 'new found religion and heresy'. The earl of Sussex, as President of the Council of the North, whose task it was to crush the rising, was convinced that the people flocked to the earls because 'they like so well their cause of religion'. The small impact that the Elizabethan religious settlement made on the religious conservatism of the North has been emphasised by recent historians.[9] In 1566, Cecil had reckoned that two-thirds of the northern justices of the peace were Catholic. Ralph Sadler, in a report to Cecil in December 1569, explained why the earl of Sussex, in quelling the rebellion, could not fully trust his forces in open conflict with the rebels.[10]

While the religious character of the rebellion has been much commented on, it is clear that there was still a great deal of uncertainty and ambiguity among the rebels, as many were torn between habits of obedience to the sovereign and their traditional loyalty to the old religion.

The consequences

While the events of the rebellion were remarkably non-violent, its suppression was less of a campaign than a military demonstration. The government was fortunate because the rising was based away from major centres of population. Moreover, it took place before Catholic reforms brought about by the Counter Reformation in Europe had time to take root in the English Catholic community. In the end, Sussex's steady loyalty and the fickleness of Norfolk proved valuable assets to the government. In the aftermath of the rebellion, many of the leaders escaped abroad, living as pensioners of Spain in the Netherlands. Eight were captured and executed at Tyburn in 1570. Others purchased their lives by forfeiting their lands and goods to the crown.

Perhaps the real significance of the Northern Rebellion lay in that the papacy, which had withheld its hand for a decade, now responded to the English situation by issuing a bull of excommunication and deposition. This was *Regnans in excelsis*, issued in March 1570 and received in England in May, which stated that the queen was formally deposed and the bonds of obedience to her on the part of her Catholic subjects dissolved. And, furthermore, the Catholic princes of Europe were to exert themselves to act against the heretic queen. All of this changed the nature of the Catholic threat. One of the Catholic powers might well put the bull into effect.[11] There was the growing crisis in the Netherlands which could easily bring England into a confrontation with Spain. And, as John Knox, writing to Cecil, reminded him (which was hardly necessary), the Queen of Scots, then in captivity in England was the Catholic claimant for the crown and the focus of all conspiracies against the whole regime. Knox wrote, 'If you strike not at the root, the branches that appear to be broken will bud again with greater force.'[12] And, finally, in the stepping up of the Catholic threat, the first missionaries from Douai began their underground ministries in 1574; by 1580 there were about a hundred of them.[13]

Harsher measures, therefore, against her Catholic subjects were now found to be necessary. In 1571, it was made treasonable to declare that Elizabeth should not be queen or that she was a heretic or schismatic. Later, legislation would make it treasonable to convert or be converted to Catholicism and in 1585 all Catholic priests had to leave the realm within 40 days or else pay the penalty of treason. In 1581, all fines imposed on recusants, that is on those who refused to attend Anglican services, were raised to £20 a month. In 1559, these fines had been a shilling a week. The recusancy fines reduced many of the richer landed Catholic families to penury.[14] In general, the vastly increased fines were not widely imposed, but used to intimidate Catholics into conformity. The persecution varied in intensity with the political climate and, in the face of parliament's demands for stronger action, Elizabeth temporised. The treason laws triggered by the papal bull threw the Catholic nobility and gentry into a conflict of loyalties.

Catholic martyrs

Elizabeth and Cecil hoped that, once deprived of its priests, banned from the schools and universities and cut off from continental support, Catholicism would die out; the very thing the Douai priests feared. Because the Catholic revival coincided with the rise of militant puritanism, Elizabethan so-called religious toleration was tested to the full. At first, priests and Catholics were imprisoned, but the first martyr executed under the treason law of 1571 was the Catholic priest, Cuthbert Mayne, in 1577. This was because his accusers connected his ministry in Cornwall with traitorous dealings with the Spanish and, in 1579, two Douai priests followed Mayne to the scaffold. The Jesuit mission in the summer of 1580, led by Edmund Campion and Robert Parsons, meant that the missionary effort in England was being largely directed by this religious order and it spurred the government on to the more severe anti-Catholic legislation discussed above. From 1581, the racking and executions multiplied to an overall total of perhaps 250 in the reign as a whole. No Catholics were burnt for heresy. Campion's trial and his death by hanging in 1581 is often used by historians to illustrate the strength and the weakness of the government's position, for the necessary measures to guard the nation against foreign intervention inevitably turned Catholics, loyal to the queen, into criminal traitors. In the light of Campion's faith and religious courage, the necessary political anxiety of the government appeared a mean and shabby stance.[15] But as always in the late-sixteenth century, one man's religion was another man's treason. Campion, like others, re-affirmed on the scaffold what he repeatedly urged during his trial. He declared, 'If you esteem my religion treason then am I guilty; as for other treason, I never committed any, God is my judge.' He then wished the queen 'a long quiet reign with all prosperity'. In the coming crisis with Spain the English Catholic community were loyal subjects, and none rebelled in the Armada year of 1588.

The international scene

Events abroad from 1568 to 1572 drew Elizabeth away from insular problems into a turbulent foreign policy; peace by diplomacy was wearing thin and came to the point of failure by 1585.[16] Cordial relations existed between Philip and Elizabeth and the growing hostility was not, at first, caused by a new hard-line Catholic attitude in Spain towards England. Philip was still anxious to get English help in his wars against France and this Elizabeth encouraged by her deceitful reception of his tentative offers of marriage. Anglo-Spanish hostility developed because of events in the Netherlands, where Spain was embroiled in war and because Elizabeth was involved in helping the French Protestants, the Huguenots, in France, when that country was about to be torn apart in half-a-century of civil war.[17]

Elizabeth's council was deeply divided: Cecil urged continued aid to the Huguenots while his opponents, Norfolk and Leicester, brought up the spectre of simultaneous war with both France and Spain. They counselled peace with Philip and the abandonment of the continental Protestants. Elizabeth was torn between her distaste for all rebels, not wanting to be identified as the religious champion of continental Protestantism, and the clearly perceived dangers in the huge Spanish military presence of about 50,000 troops under the duke of Alva in the Netherlands. Once his men had restored order and wiped out Protestantism there, might he not take advantage of the good harbours and the prevailing winds and use his base in the Netherlands as a staging post for the invasion of heretical England? In the event, Spain would wage a costly war of suppression for 82 years against the Dutch struggle for independence. But, for Elizabeth, war at that time with the most powerful state in western Europe was out of the question. The queen hated the expense of war and the taxation it would mean, and to her a war postponed might be a war averted. Moreover, she might be helping France if she resisted Spain. On the other hand, she knew that to leave Spain's powerful position in the Netherlands unchallenged would menace England. Here lay Elizabeth's dilemma. She constantly complained about the expense of Sir Francis Walsingham's spy service, the corruption in the expeditionary forces sent into Ireland at various times, and wrangled over the grants of money sent to support the Dublin administration and loans sent to help foreign Protestants.[18] (On Ireland, see Document 7.5 on p. 83 and note 21 on p. 85.) Indirect and desultory help was sent to continental co-religionists such as to the beleaguered Huguenots at La Rochelle, and her seamen like Hawkins and Drake were encouraged to break Spain's trading monopoly by acts of harassment against Spanish sea-power.[19] Between 1568 and 1585, there was an increase in these acts of piracy to which Elizabeth never gave official sanction. Instead, she

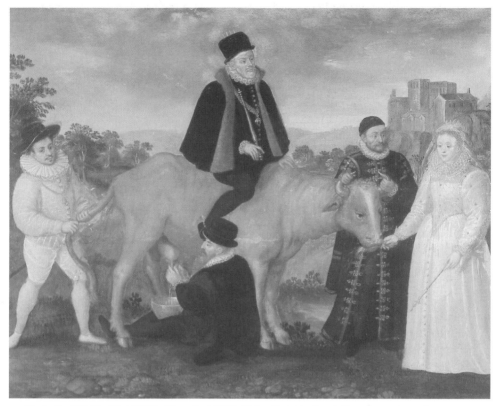

Portrait of Philip II by Philip Moro (*c.* 1570). This allegorical painting shows how dangerous the complex problems presented to Elizabeth by the Netherlands really were. Philip II, the rightful ruler of the Netherlands, is riding a cow but draws blood with his spur while his commander in the Netherlands, the duke of Alva, is milking the cow. William of Orange, the Protestant leader of the rebels, offers the cow for Elizabeth to feed. The duke of Anjou (brother of the French king) pulls the cow's tail indicating that his support for the rebels (which Elizabeth tried to encourage) disguises the self-interest of France.

characteristically turned a blind eye and pocketed the proceeds of the raids. Many of these were on the Spanish bullion ships sailing from the gold and silver mines of South America destined to pay Alva's troops. As a result, Philip II placed an embargo on all English property in the Netherlands.

The year 1572 was crucial in the Dutch resistance; the conflict then broke out into open war. William, prince of Orange, had hoped for French help, but the religious crisis in France, culminating in the massacre of the Huguenots on St Bartholomew's Day in August, destroyed Protestant influence at the French court. He had no other base than the towns of Brill and Flushing, occupied by the Sea Beggars, from which to meet the Spanish effort at reconquest. It was from there, too, that English troops in the Netherlands saw their first active service, but by 1574 most of them had been discharged. But, as long as the Dutch could hold out, Philip would hesitate to attack England. Knowing this, Elizabeth resisted the temptation, urged on her by Walsingham and Leicester, to declare openly for the Dutch. In 1576, she did give succour to the refugees from the sack of Antwerp – an episode that united the Netherland provinces against the Spanish cruelty. But, in 1578, a new Spanish army under the duke of Parma began a steady campaign of reconquest. For the next seven years, the fortunes of the Dutch rebels deteriorated, despite help from Elizabeth; she sent a contingent of troops under Sir John Norris, which was helped by Roger Williams and his men, as they deserted from the Spanish army in which they were serving as mercenaries.

Meanwhile, in the Elizabethan council, advice to the queen was still divided between the 'war party' under Walsingham and Leicester and the 'peace party' headed by the cautious and now ageing William Cecil, Lord Burghley. As for Elizabeth, her tortuous policy continued: she encouraged France to aid the rebels and at the same time tried to deter the Dutch from accepting French help at too great a political price. However, the air cleared and decisions had to be made by the summer of 1585, when Henry III of France, far from helping the rebels, declared himself the ally of Philip of Spain. Elizabeth was forced to make a decision and at Nonsuch Palace, on 10 August 1585, a treaty was signed between English and Dutch negotiators. England agreed to supply 5,000 foot and 1,000 horse troops under the earl of Leicester, and £126,000 per annum for their maintenance as long as the war lasted. In addition, as security for the repayment of English expenditure, the towns of Brill and Flushing were to be garrisoned by English troops. Leicester made himself Governor General of the Provinces, a huge political blunder that implied that Elizabeth was their sovereign, and he, her Viceroy. Furthermore, his military strategy, in going on the full offensive, was unwelcome to the Dutch leaders. But the two years he spent in the Netherlands were not totally wasted. After all, the defence of Holland and Zeeland and the battle at Zutphen in which Sir Philip Sidney died were victories, even though Parma remained supreme.

The Spanish response to England openly aiding her rebels and the fear that Walsingham might eventually secure a general Protestant alliance, resulted in much anger and retaliation. It is at this stage that Philip offered assistance to English and Irish Catholics, allowed the Spanish Inquisition a free hand against Protestant Englishmen throughout his empire, and engineered a series of plots to dethrone Elizabeth and make Mary Stuart queen of England. His actions triggered the Ridolfi Plot in 1571, the Throckmorton plot in 1583 and the Babington Conspiracy of 1586, which was instrumental in leading to the execution of Mary Stuart in 1587. Philip's policy took on the ethos of a religious crusade, particularly after Pius V's excommunication of the queen in *Regnans in excelsis*.

The maritime offensive against Philip's shipping (particularly the well-known 'singeing of the king of Spain's beard', Drake's brilliantly successful attack on the ships and stores being prepared for 'The Enterprise of England' in the early summer of 1587) and the execution of the Scots queen hastened on the mounting of the celebrated Armada.

The execution of Mary Queen of Scots

Mary was executed on 8 February 1587 at Fotheringhay Castle as she read her prayers out loud to silence the ministrations of the Protestant chaplain.[20] Elizabeth's hesitancy to sign the death warrant is well known; she also knew that both Scotland and France would do little more than protest. She was also aware that Philip II of Spain's claim to the English throne was now as sound as that of the heretical James VI of Scotland, Mary's son who was carefully brought up in the Protestant faith. Up to the last minute before the launch of the Armada Enterprise, the queen continued peace negotiations, hoping that Philip might drop the proposed design; negotiation gave her time, in any case, to strengthen defences on land and to fit out the fleet. On 28 May 1588, the Armada set out from Lisbon with its 130 ships, 2,400 guns and 30,000 men; the largest fighting force on the Atlantic until the English fleets were assembled later in the year.

Elizabeth I, 1558–88

7.1 Some aspects of Elizabeth's religious settlement

Count von Helffstein, the Imperial envoy, to the Emperor Ferdinand I, 16 March 1559 (letter)

From the very beginning of her reign she has treated all religious questions with so much caution and incredible prudence that she seems both to protect the Catholic religion and at the same time not entirely to condemn or outwardly reject the new Reformation . . . In my opinion a very prudent action, intended to keep the adherents of both creeds in subjection, for the less she ruffles them at the beginning of her reign the more easily she will enthral them later on.

Source: V. von Klarwill (ed.), *Queen Elizabeth and some foreigners*, tr. by T. N. Nash, London, 1928, p. 47

Details of Elizabeth's coronation, held on 15 January 1559 from the Calendar of state papers*. This was the last coronation ceremony to be conducted in Latin and took place before parliament met to settle religion and the new Prayer Book.*

The service concluded with the saying of Mass by Bishop Oglethorpe. Both epistle and gospel were read in English as well as in Latin . . . Elizabeth left her throne to make her offertory on her knees before the high altar and to kiss the paten . . . Instead of returning to her throne, as the rubrics stated, she withdrew to a traverse [secluded pew] in St Edward's Chapel where she remained till the consecration of the elements and the elevation of the host were completed.

Source: N. William, *Elizabeth Queen of England*, London, 1967

The Oath of Supremacy, 1559

I . . . do utterly testify and declare in my conscience that the Queen's Highness is the only supreme governor of this realm and of all other her Highness' dominions and countries, as well in all spiritual or ecclesiastical things or causes as temporal, and that no foreign prince, person, prelate, state or potentate hath or ought to have any jurisdiction, power, superiority, pre-eminence or authority ecclesiastical or spiritual within this realm and therefore I do utterly renounce and forsake all foreign jurisdictions . . . and do promise that from henceforth I shall bear faith and true allegiance to the Queen's Highness, her heirs and lawful successors . . . so help me God and by the contents of this Book.

Source: A. Landers et al. (eds.) *Statutes of the realm*, vol. 4, p. 352, I Elizabeth, c. 1, London, 1810–28

William Cecil, Lord Burghley writing on the royal service to his son, Robert (letters)

[1580s]

Towards thy superiors be humble yet generous, with thy equals familiar yet respective; towards inferiors show much humility and some familiarity . . . the first prepares the way to advancement; the second makes thee known for a man well bred, the third gains a good report which once gotten may be safely kept . . . yet do I advise thee not to affect nor to neglect popularity too much. Seek not to be E [Essex] and shun to be R [Ralegh] . . . Serve God by serving the Queen for all other service is indeed bondage to the devil.

Source: L. B. Wright (ed.), *Advice to a son*, New York, 1962, pp. 12–13

[23 March 1596]

I do hold and will always, this course in such matters as I differ in opinion from her Majesty; as long as I may be allowed to give advice, I will not change my opinion by affirming the contrary, for that were to offend God, to whom I am sworn first; but as a servant I will obey her Majesty's commandment . . . presuming that she be God's chief minister here it shall be God's will to have her commandments obeyed . . . after that I have performed my duty as a councillor and shall in my heart wish her commandments to have such good successes as I am sure she intendeth.

Source: T. Wright (ed.), *Queen Elizabeth and her times*, vol. 2, London, 1838, p. 457

7.2 Puritan and papist opposition

Lord Burghley to Archbishop Whitgift, 1 July 1584 (letter)

My good lord I am come to the sight of an instrument of twenty-four articles of great length and curiosity, found in a Romish style, to examine all manner of ministers . . . which articles are entitled, *apud Lambeth*, May 1584 to be executed *ex officio mero* etc [given at Lambeth and to be carried out to the letter] . . . I find them so full of branches and circumstances as I think the inquisitors of Spain use not so many questions to comprehend and trap their preys.

Surely under your grace's correction this judicial and canonical sifting of poor ministers is not to edify or reform . . . they ought not to answer all these nice points except they were notorious offenders in papistry or heresy . . . it is all rather a device to seek out offenders than to reform any.

Source: J. Strype, *The life and acts of John Whitgift*, vol. 3, Oxford, 1822, pp. 105–106

7.3 The Northern Rebellion, 1569

The proclamation of the rebellious earls

Thomas, Earl of Northumberland and Charles, Earl of Westmorland, the queen's most true and lawful subjects and to all her highness's people sendeth greeting: Whereas divers new set up nobles about the Queen's Majesty have and do daily, not only go about to overthrow and put down the ancient nobility of this realm but have also misused the Queen's own person and have also by the space of twelve years now past set up and maintained a new found religion and heresy contrary to God's word. For the amending and redressing thereof divers foreign powers do purpose shortly to invade this realm which will be to our utter destruction if we do not speedily forfend the same . . . we should go about and amend and redress ourselves . . . which if we do not . . . we should all be made slaves and bondsmen to them . . . we will and require each and every of you as your duty to God for the setting forth of his true and Catholic religion . . . come and resort unto us with all speed with all the armour and furniture as you or any of you have.

Source: C. Sharp (ed.), *Memorials of the rebellion of 1569*, (ed. from B. L. Harleian MS 6990, fo. 44), London, 1840, p. 42

7.4 An attack on episcopacy and plans for a Presbyterian church

The Second admonition to parliament, *1572*

You must repeal your statutes whereby you have authorised ministry that now is . . . appointing an order to ordain ministers which is clean differing from the Scriptures . . . instead when a parish is destitute of a pastor or teacher . . . procure from one of the universities a man learned and of good report, whom after trial of his gifts and after be certified of the parish's liking . . . and after prayer, fasting and sermon according to the example of Scriptures made by the congregation to God that it would please Him to direct them in their choice and bless the man whom they shall choose . . . the elders will lay their hands on him to signify that he is lawfully called to that parish to be their pastor.

Source: J. R. Tanner, *Tudor constitutional documents*, Cambridge, 2nd edn, 1930, pp. 167–70

7.5 Concerning the justice of the war in Ireland for the Faith, 1579

From 1569 to 1573 and again from 1579 to 1583 the Irish province of Munster was in a state of rebellion led by James Fitzmaurice Fitzgerald, a cousin of the earl of Desmond. These two periods of unrest are called the First and Second Desmond Rebellions. This is the proclamation of James Fitzmaurice Fitzgerald, on the outbreak of the second rebellion[21]

This war is undertaken for the defence of the Catholic religion against the heretics. Pope Gregory XIII hath chosen us for general captain in this same war as it appeareth at large by his own letters patent which thing he did so much rather because his predecessor Pius V had before deprived Elizabeth, the patroness of the aforesaid heresies, of all royal power and dominion . . . therefore we fight not against the lawful sceptre and honourable throne of England, but against a tyrant which refuseth to hear Christ speaking by his vicar.

Source: *The calendar of Carew* MSS, I, 400

7.6 Leicester's expedition to the Netherlands, December 1585

His instructions from the queen's commission to Leicester

To have care that her Majesty's subjects serving under his lordship may be well governed and to use all good means to redress the confused government of those countries . . . his lordship is directed to bend his course, during his charge there, rather to make a defensive than an offensive war, and not in any sort to hazard a battle without great advantage . . . to work amongst them a fair unity for their own defence in liberal taxation and good husbanding of their contributions for the more speedy attaining of a peace.

Source: J. Bruce (ed.), *Correspondence of Robert Dudley, earl of Leicester, 1585–86*, Camden Society, vol. 27, London, 1844, pp. 12–15

Document case-study questions

1 The five documents in 7.1 concern the religious settlement of 1559–60. How far do they help to explain Elizabeth's cautious approach to religion?

2 In what respects does 7.2 confirm Elizabeth's view that she did not want 'to open windows into men's souls'?

3 What were the main religious objections to the Elizabethan church settlement according to 7.4?

4 How far was the Northern Rebellion of 1569–70 a matter of religion or loss of political influence? Use 7.3 to support your argument.

5 The tone of 7.5 differs from that of 7.3 in several important respects. In what ways and why?

6 What instructions was the earl of Leicester given for his expedition to the Netherlands and why? Use 7.6. to support your argument.

Notes and references

1 In October 1562, Elizabeth nearly died of smallpox; it was the only serious illness of her life.

2 S. T. Bindoff, *Tudor England*, London, 1963 edn, p. 183.

3 Note how Parker's consecration as archbishop of Canterbury on 17 December 1559 was carried out by the four surviving Marian bishops, although they were without sees. A link between the old and the new succession of clerical orders in the church of England was, therefore, maintained. The role of the episcopate under Elizabeth is a difficult, but fascinating, religious and political topic. See D. MacCullough, *Thomas Cranmer, a life*, Yale, 1997.

4 Hooker's work, published from 1594, is the chief apologia for Anglicanism. It makes strong statements against Presbyterianism, and presents arguments that justify the Elizabethan church settlement and the episcopacy. Furthermore the *Laws of ecclesiastical polity* argued that Scripture was not the only basis for the church's teaching, as human reasoning, ecclesiastical tradition and the authority of the state are also important.

5 See under parliament in the Select bibliography.

6 N. L. Jones, *Faith by statute: parliament and the settlement of religion*, London, 1982.

7 Peter Wentworth, who died in the Tower in 1596, was more a martyr to his persistent defence of the right of an MP to speak freely in the House of Commons, than to puritanism, although he became the standard bearer of liberty for the puritans in parliament.

8 Cartwright had been dismissed from his Chair of Divinity at Cambridge on account of his critical lectures on the Established church. Both there, and in the *Second admonition*, the ignorance and incompetence of the clergy, especially their ability to preach, were attacked.

9 See such authors as C. Haigh, P. Williams, J. Guy and A. G. Dickens in the Select bibliography.

10 See document 7.3 in this chapter.

11 The Ridolfi plot in March 1571 was the result of the bull; see Bindoff, *Tudor England*, ch. vii.

12 Quoted in A. Fletcher, *Tudor rebellions*, Harlow, 1983.

13 Between 1568 and 1603, 803 seminary priests were trained, largely by the Jesuits. Of these, 649 were sent into England, and about 130 of these were executed. St Ignatius of Loyola founded the Society of Jesus (the Jesuits) to help in the reform of Catholicism. They were often regarded as the shock troops of the pope.

14 There is a vast literature on recusancy notably in the publications of the Catholic Records Society and the *Journal of recusant history*. For one example of how the recusancy laws operated in one shire, see J. J. N. McGurk, 'Lieutenancy and Catholic recusants in Elizabethan Kent', in *Journal of recusant history* (February 1974). For the recent research work on Catholic survivalism, see under E. Duffy, and C. Haigh in the Select bibliography.

15 There are many biographies, but see E. Waugh, *Edmund Campion*, London, 1947.

16 Elizabeth's foreign policy is immensely complex. For a brief analysis, see S. Doran, *England and Europe*, Harlow, 1986, and for a full discussion see the two works by R. B. Wernham and those of W. T. MacCaffrey in the Select bibliography.

17 Note that it was the French who first challenged Spanish preserves, not only in Italy and the Netherlands but also in the Atlantic and the Caribbean. See the masterly essays in G. Parker, *Spain and the Netherlands – ten studies, 1559–1659*, London, 1979.

18 There are about 70 biographies of Elizabeth and the latest are not always the best, but see W. T. MacCaffrey, *Elizabeth I*, London, 1993; and C. Haigh (ed.), *The reign of Elizabeth I*, London, 1984, as well as assessments of the queen's character in the general texts on Elizabethan England.

19 See for example, G. D. Ramsay, *The queen's merchants and the Revolt of the Netherlands*, Manchester, 1986, and the same author's *English overseas trade during the centuries of emergence*, London, 1957.

20 He was the Dean of Peterborough to whom Mary is reported to have said, 'Mr Dean, I am a Catholic, and must die a Catholic. It is useless to attempt to move me, and your prayers will avail me but little.'

21 Sir James Fitzmaurice Fitzgerald headed an Old English revolt in defence of Catholicism and of ancestral properties. They were joined by the Gaelic lords like MacCarthy Mór because they, too, had suffered confiscations of lands at the hand of the New English adventurers. The revolt was very severely crushed by Carew, aided by Gilbert, Hawkins, Frobisher and Ralegh (1573–74). Fitzmaurice escaped to the courts of Europe to collect an invading force

and, with Spanish and Italian help, landed in Kerry in July 1579. This second attempt was put down with equal severity; the insurgents were abandoned by Philip II of Spain; the 25th earl of Desmond was killed and all Munster was quiet by 1583. See John McGurk, 'The fall of the noble house of Desmond 1579–1583', in *History today*, vol. 29, London (1979).

8 Elizabeth I: the later years, 1588–1603

The Armada

The reasons for the Armada and open war with Spain are clear: the execution of Mary Stuart in February 1587 united the Catholic forces in Europe sufficiently to make Philip's 'Enterprise of England' a possibility; in August 1587, Leicester's mission to the Netherlands had largely failed while the duke of Parma was partially successful against the Huguenots in parts of France and the Netherlands; in France, the Catholic Henry of Guise had control of Paris over his rivals for the throne, Henry Valois and Henry of Navarre (later Henry IV of France). Guise, one of the strongest members of the Catholic League, was in the pay of Spain. Philip, confident of French support and the unlikelihood of hindrance from the Netherlands, was in a good position to strike.

Preparations on both sides went forward throughout the autumn and winter of 1587. In England, Sir John Hawkins, as Treasurer of the Navy and main adviser to Elizabeth on naval matters, had carried out a revolution in the number, type and serviceability of ships of war. Instead of being floating fortresses, designed for the grappling and boarding of enemy vessels in hand-to-hand combat, these became floating gun platforms, light and speedy and capable of long-range engagement. Hawkins had also reformed the administration, eliminating waste and corruption, differentiating the duties of seamen and soldiers and appointing their captains on merit. Drake's raids on Cape St Vincent and Cadiz caused the loss of vital Spanish supplies and left a number of Spanish ships unseaworthy. Moreover, the death in February of the Spanish admiral, Santa Cruz, lowered morale. But, by May, under the duke of Medina-Sidonia, the Armada was ready for the Enterprise; its coming was dreaded in England.

Elizabeth had avoided open warfare for 30 years and had saved England from foreign domination; by 1588 the nation was violently opposed to Spain and Catholicism. If Spain defeated England, then Protestantism in Europe would suffer a severe blow. It now seemed likely that Henry of Guise would be king of France and that Europe would be united by a common religion. Prophecies, almanacs and sermons predicting the end of Elizabeth, the English Jezebel, were rife; 1588 was to be the year of doom. In England, rapid preparations for defence went on, particularly on the Thames and south coast and, to their chagrin, prominent Catholics were put under house arrest.[1]

The actual events of the victory, the naval actions in the Channel and the wrecking of the remnants of the Spanish ships off the Scottish and Irish coasts are well known. The effects are, however, still controversial. Certainly, the victory saved England and Protestantism at the time, but it only began a war which outlived Elizabeth. Invasion scares continued and Ireland's Nine Years' War (1594–1603) went bravely on consuming men, horses and treasure to a greater extent than anywhere else. This war began as an Ulster rebellion under Hugh O'Neill, earl of Tyrone in 1594, but quickly involved the whole of Ireland. Spain sent money and arms until, in 1601, 4,000 Spanish troops were to land at Kinsale in Munster where they and their Irish allies were defeated by the Lord Deputy, Mountjoy. Elizabeth's involvement in the Netherlands continued to soak up men and money and she continued to support Henry of Navarre and the French Huguenots until 1593; over £300,000, or more than a year's revenue, was sent to France in the five years after the Armada. Taxes were raised, crown lands sold, loans demanded and the shires and towns harassed for able-bodied men and more monies to equip and send out the levies to the wars. Plague and bad harvests and the deaths of many of the queen's older counsellors – like Leicester, Knollys and Hatton, the war leaders Drake, Hawkins and Frobisher, as well as Walsingham and, in 1598, Burghley himself – all conspired to make the 1590s a decade of disillusionment and disappointment. The lack of economic resources alone made nonsense of the war party's plans to carry the war into Spain.

With the defeat of the Armada, Spain was put on the defensive and no longer regarded by Rome as the spearhead of the Counter Reformation. Pope Sixtus V, however, made no secret of his admiration for Elizabeth, and for Drake. He knew that his own independence could have been threatened by an overambitious Spain. But, by 1603, while the sovereignty over Ireland had been maintained at a grim price, Spain had not lost a single overseas outpost to England even though, as a world power, it had lost its primacy and prestige. The expedition under Drake and Norris in 1589 to invade and liberate Portugal from the Spanish was a failure, and Essex and Ralegh's voyage to the Azores in 1597 was another. In 1598, Philip II died; and when Henry of Navarre became king of France, the French wars of religion became part of the Anglo-Spanish conflict. England continued to aid the Protestant Dutch, and Spain sent help to the Catholic Guises in France. The war in Ireland absorbed all other efforts, proving a greater strain on the treasury than any other theatre of war. Essex with a formidable army failed in Ireland, and his successor, Mountjoy, took several years to effect the final reconquest with the surrender of O'Neill in 1603.

The economy

The economic effects of the conflict with Spain and with Ireland certainly had constitutional implications, particularly on relations between the crown and parliament, the gentry class and the common people. In a revealing comment before his death in 1598, Burghley warned of 'the common people of England, inclinable to sedition if they be oppressed with extraordinary payments' and 'that there was an inbred disaffection in the vulgar towards the nobility'. Echoes of this disaffection can be heard in the parliamentary debates for additional subsidies at the end of the reign.

How confident was the late-Elizabethan government about its powers to coerce its own subjects? Parliamentary grants were increasingly requested, which meant a rise in both indirect and direct taxation. From 1589 to 1603, the amount raised was three times the amount raised in the previous thirty years. Finance was a constant source of conflict between the queen and her council and the last parliaments of the reign; so too was her suppression of church bills, dealing with all manner of ecclesiastical discipline, dogma and church rights, and the monopolies (grants giving the sole right to make or sell a certain commodity) by which she rewarded officials and favourites. Her council was also clamorous against all other prerogative courts – such as the Court of High Commission, the Admiral's Court, the Council of the North, the Court of Wards and the Court of Requests. Such quarrels raised two very important questions: firstly on the nature and extent of parliamentary liberty, which came to a head in the Peter Wentworth case on parliamentary free speech, and secondly on the claim that there was only one sovereign rule, that of parliament and the common law of the land, often voiced in the Commons. In an angry session of 1597 to 1598, the queen vetoed ten bills, and in 1601 the sessions proved more tumultuous, 'more fit for a grammar school', said Sir Robert Cecil, 'than a court of parliament' while the Commons 'hawked, spat and hemmed'. In the debates over monopolies, many of them concerning necessities like salt, coal and leather, one member asked 'Is not bread there?' 'What purpose is it', said another, 'to do anything with act of parliament when the queen will undo the same by her prerogative?' In the event she did make a graceful retreat on the matter of monopolies, withdrawing those she had allowed 'for lack of true information' such as those on starch, bottles and salt. But this abuse of the prerogative as perks for courtiers became worse under James I.

From the 1590s, parliament voted multiple subsidies (or taxes), four, for example, in 1601, when the Irish war was at its height; but in all of these debates there were attacks on the royal methods of raising money, particularly on Wardship, purveyance and monopolies, as well as the increased taxation on the shires due to the re-arming of the militia with up-to-date firearms.[2] The organisation of the shire militias under lords lieutenants centralised defence under the crown.

The interruption of trade resulting from the war on the high seas badly affected the well-being of the small trader and especially the many engaged in the cloth industry; the loss of Antwerp as an entrepot was serious, but the centralisation of so much trade into the hands of the large London companies also hit the cottage industries and small traders. Moreover, the plagues and bad harvests of the 1590s which sent up the price of corn and, therefore, of bread to unprecedented levels greatly affected the lower classes of society; in some areas there were famine conditions.[3]

From the detailed evidence it is clear that not everyone suffered in the 1590s; many sectors of the community prospered in wartime. This was especially true of those with influential posts in the expeditionary forces in the army and navy, and in all the areas to do with supplying the forces: food, clothing, munitions and, above all, shipping. The economic historians of the period show how the gentry and wealthier yeomanry continued to become wealthier and point to the rebuilding of the great manors and houses throughout many shires. There can be little doubt of the significant growth in domestic luxuries among the new rich. Privateering and long-distance trade also flourished. While the lower sectors of the realm suffered economic hardships, the rich were growing richer and not only on the profits of land as before. Many grew wealthy from mining and metal-lurgy and the opening up of new industries, so much so that a few economic historians would put the origins of the industrial revolution in the latter years of Elizabeth.[4]

The entire population of late Elizabethan England was probably less than four million by 1603. The aristocracy and lesser gentry consisted of about 2,000 families. The yeomen and the wealthier peasantry in the countryside and the substantial merchants of the towns, especially port towns, all began to take part in central and local government. Hence, aristocracy, gentry and the rising middle class of yeomen and merchants became a governing class which was representative of only about ten per cent of the population. Politics was thus the art of the possible in managing this governing class. It was done to a great extent by patronage – the granting of appointments, privileges, exemptions, honours – rewards that were in the queen's gift and in the hands of many courtiers who had access to her. In the competition for jobs, status and power, factions clearly emerged but they were far from being political parties. They were neither firm nor permanent nor possessed of one ideology of government. Elizabeth's system was open-ended, in which men of ability like Ralegh and Essex could rise, but equally fall even at the frown of the prince, or as in Ralegh's case by an unfortunate marriage.

How did the queen manage the governing classes? How did England escape foreign invasion, religious warfare, civil war, social unrest, on any large scale, and bankruptcy in the queen's reign? These are questions which have exercised many. A satisfactory answer may not be possible, but by reading and reflecting on the sources of the 1590s some compromise answers may be achieved.

Parliament, puritans and opposition to the queen

Parliament

The queen and the privy council, the main instruments of Elizabethan government, worked continuously. By contrast, parliament met when called, therefore occasionally and for brief sessions at a time. Throughout a reign of 44 years, Elizabeth called ten parliaments with a total of 13 sessions, and a session was usually less than a ten-week period. Parliament was, therefore, active for less than three years during the reign. It is true that the queen alone could summon, prorogue and dissolve parliaments, but she needed parliament to make laws and, above all, to raise taxes. The executive's, or the government's, need for money largely explains why they were summoned at all.

However, the parliament of 1586 was called neither to make laws nor vote money; instead its purpose was 'rare and extraordinary and of great weight, great peril and dangerous consequence' as the Lord Chancellor, Sir Thomas Bromley, said in the opening speech. Its purpose was nothing less than to consider what to do about Mary Queen of Scots' clear involvement in the Babington Conspiracy. This was not to say that Elizabeth sought parliamentary sanction for her execution, as the formal death sentence had already been passed. Parliament simply published the decision taken.

In the mounting costs of the war with Spain in the 1590s, the last three parliaments of the reign were specifically called to make large financial grants, triple subsidies, in fact, in 1593 and 1597 to fund the hostilities in the Netherlands, France and Ireland.[5] In 12 out of the 13 sessions of the Elizabethan parliaments, the government asked for money and in six sessions it had important legislation to put through.[6]

It can no longer be maintained that the queen and council members used crude electoral engineering to 'pack' parliaments with favourites to get a 'consensus' for legislation and taxation. But there was a powerful nucleus of officials, and many MPs gained their seats from the patronage of peers and courtiers, many of whom sat in every House of Commons during the period. The crown could normally rely on their support. The queen could interfere directly and sometimes did, especially when she considered a bill or a discussion to be a matter in her own prerogative, such as religion, her marriage and the succession. Her usual combination of tact and influence meant that she got her way.[7] Elizabeth, therefore, controlled the workings of parliament by use of the royal veto, direct interventions to stay bills being discussed, and drastically, the imprisonment of members.

However, some see in her speeches and messages to both Houses a charm and a rapport that worked; there is much 'hearty and loving thanks' to 'religious, godly and obedient subjects' and dramatic and charming gestures when she assented to bills. But all that personal charm and magic was wearing thin in the 1590s.

In general, there was a widening rift in the relations between the queen and her parliaments in the last years of her reign. There had also been differences before 1588 in Peter Wentworth's championship of the parliamentary privilege of free speech, for example. Moreover, his outspoken comments on religion had been a particular thorn in the side of the crown in the 1570s. But those quarrels over religion, the church, the marriage and the succession and even the position of Mary Queen of Scots had receded as the more immediate threat to national security from Spain and the Catholic forces in Europe grew larger. The defeat of the Armada did not remove that threat, but it did afford a breathing space in which domestic issues were re-opened by the most powerful sector, the landed gentry, who were after all represented in parliament.[8] In Elizabeth's last years, therefore, her relations with parliament became more turbulent. Members

QUEEN ELIZABETH IN PARLIAMENT

A. *Ld Chancellor* B. *Marquess*, *Earles &c* C. *Barons* D. *Bishops* E. *Iudges* F. *Masters of Chancery* G. *Clerks* H. *Speaker of ye Comons* I. *Black Rod* K. *Serieant at Armes* L. *Members of ye Commons house* M. *S.r Francis Walsingham Secretary of State*.

Queen Elizabeth I (1533–1603) in parliament (English School, sixteenth century, panel). Did the presence of the queen in parliament mean that her government was a constitutional monarchy?

increasingly demanded the right to discuss what were considered by the queen to be matters of her prerogative. In answer to the queen's tart assertion to them, 'Your privilege is Aye or No, the right to pass or veto legislation', the Commons asserted its ancient rights to freedom of speech, freedom from arrest, jurisdiction over its own members and freedom of access to the sovereign. In 1601, referring to the Commons' debate on monopolies, Sir Robert Cecil declared, 'I have been a member of this House . . . in six or seven parliaments, yet never did I see the House in so great confusion.' On that occasion, too, the queen pleaded her prerogative which she referred to as the 'fairest flower in her garden', to which she received the reply, 'God grant that the prerogative touch not our liberty.'[9]

Since parliament controlled the purse, the main cause of contention between Elizabeth and her Commons was clearly finance; she had to face the familiar problem of a static income in an inflationary age of rising costs. Many of her subjects, especially the *nouveaux riches*, were getting wealthier as the crown was growing poorer. The queen found it difficult, if not impossible, to live on and run the government with the traditional and fixed feudal revenues of the crown; parliamentary grants were increasingly needed, especially in the 1590s, with the vastly increased cost of expeditionary forces and warfare abroad and in Ireland. In the sixteenth century, it appears that parliament did not seem to make any distinction between monies granted to the crown for its own private usage and monies granted for the payment of services; for example, to the judges, officials in the army and the navy, such as the Treasurers at war in Ireland, and other grants to the Dublin administration at a time of expensive hostilities. In this period, there are many indications of why Elizabeth gained a reputation for thrift and meanness – Drake, for example, having to pay the Armada sailors out of his own pocket and Hawkins erecting almshouses in Deptford and Greenwich for his disabled sailors and soldiers.[10] The financial embarrassment of the crown was especially increased by the Nine Years' War in Ireland. Because of this, until she died, the queen had to ask parliament for more and more money as the war there dragged on. Parliament, formerly, had been willing enough to vote taxation for the necessary defence of the realm but in 1593, 1597 and from 1601 to 1603 grants were made with increasing reluctance and with much muttering about the general impoverishment of the nation at large. In fact, between 1593 and 1601, the crown asked for ten subsidies.[11]

One final significant trend needs to be noted here; the way in which the emergent committee structure in the House began to take upon itself the work of drawing up legislation. It thereby began to take the initiative in general domestic policies such as vagrancy, poverty and enclosures, all of them serious matters, out of the hands of the government.

By the end of Elizabeth's reign, the earlier warmth between queen and Commons had gone. This was noted in one of her last visits as she confirmed the Commons choice of a Speaker in 1601; as she passed the bar of the Lords' chamber, 'few said, "God Bless your Majesty" as they were wont in all great assemblies.'[12] And, in writing to the king of France, the queen remarked, 'All the fabric of my reign, little by little, is beginning to fall.' By the turn of the century she was nearing her seventieth year; and still she had yet to face the last major crisis of her life in the Irish war and the revolt of her former favourite the second earl of Essex.

Puritans

The emergence of the extreme Protestants, the puritans, has already been noted and their impact in parliament and on the Established church has, according to more modern research, likely been exaggerated.[13] However, many members of the later Elizabethan parliaments were puritan and, as long as they were happy to campaign for minor changes in the rituals of the Established church, they made little stir. But, when the more extreme demanded radical changes in the very nature and actual constitution of the national church, based as it was on episcopacy, then the crown as its Supreme Governor was forced to make a stand. Church and state were one, for whenever there was an attack on the one, there lay a threat to the other. By insisting that their ministers be elected by their congregations, on the same lines as the Scottish Presbyterian church, puritans were, in fact, demanding democracy in church government and from there it was a short step to demanding the same in the state. Many political theorists have, in fact, seen in these puritan ideals of church government an important theoretical opposition to absolutism in church and state. It is significant that Richard Hooker was especially concerned in the celebrated *Laws of ecclesiastical polity* to make an effective ideological counterattack against the puritans. Outside parliament, Archbishop Whitgift began a thorough persecution of them through the Court of High Commission. In this way, Cartwright, the author of the *Admonitions* and a leading figure in the movement, was imprisoned, and a number of separatists hanged after the scurrilous attacks from the underground press in the Marprelate Tracts on episcopacy. The slogan, ' No bishop, no king' was evidently as clear to Elizabeth I as it was to be to her successor James I.

The earl of Essex

The details of Essex's career have been well documented in most lives of the queen, and also in texts on the Tudors such as those by G. R. Elton, J. Guy, S. T. Bindoff and W. T. MacCaffrey. His unsuccessful efforts to substitute himself for the Cecils in the queen's inner circle were followed by the debacle of his Irish campaign in which he wasted vast resources against Hugh O'Neill, earl of Tyrone. He finally resorted to a rebellion in arms in the streets of London in the course of his attempt to seize control of the queen and his rivals at court. In a true historical sense, the second earl of Essex is of interest in any discussion of monarchies as he represents the last of the overmighty subjects – a theme which dominated late-medieval England and the earlier Tudor period. The wheel of history had come full circle, as Elizabeth found herself confronted, at the end of her days, with a similar task to that of her grandfather, Henry VII. This was to crush an overwhelmingly ambitious subject, who was likely to create his own following, if not his own private army, and take part in intrigues with the crown's rivals. The only difference was that, in the last days of Elizabeth, it was an open secret that her cousin, James VI of Scotland, would succeed her. Moreover, her courtiers were secretly agreed on that course of action. Some historians comment on how lucky Elizabeth was, in that the only man who had the potential to become a real threat to her regime could not draw all the elements of dissatisfaction together. If his rebellion to overthrow the queen and Cecil had attracted popular support, it would have been a political catastrophe for the realm. Indeed, Sir Robert Cecil, after Essex's failed revolt, was already in touch with the Scots king, for Cecil knew, in the last illness of the dying queen, that James would soon be his new master. Others like Ralegh, Lord Cobham and Northumberland were also currying favour with James. It was an anxious time; the Jesuit, Robert Parsons, who had escaped to France a year after the arrest of Campion had publicised the rightful claim of the Spanish infanta to the English succession, causing fears of intervention or at least local uprisings on the death of the queen. None of this happened; the new king of England was proclaimed when the end came for Elizabeth on 24 March 1603. James VI of Scotland set out from Edinburgh to become also James I of England, Wales and Ireland.

For almost 45 years, Elizabeth's decisions had shaped the public life of the realm. She had inherited a monarchy that allowed for strongly centralised leadership backed up by a long-established series of courts and an efficient bureaucracy; the use she had made of this legacy of government by council, courts and parliament was masterly. This is particularly true as the domestic scene was often clouded and the international one, in which there was little room for manoeuvre, downright dangerous.

Local government and administration

The complex and controversial subject of local government and administration during Elizabeth's reign has generated a vast amount of local research, virtually shire-by-shire, since the 1960s.

The majority of the queen's subjects had no direct contact with the central authorities, but they could hardly avoid local officials, especially the justices of the peace, the deputy sheriffs and deputy lieutenants and commissioners, in the course of their many duties. These could include such things as the discovery of recusants, the collection of the subsidies and other taxes, not to mention the putting into effect of a host of parliamentary statutes. Although the lords lieutenants and the justices of the peace were the key local government officers, the traditional work of the high sheriff and his deputy continued throughout the queen's reign.

The sheriff

The sheriff presided over the monthly meetings of the county court. He also had duties at the assizes and quarter sessions courts, such as the carrying out of sentences in delivering convicted prisoners safely from the courts to gaol, custody of the county gaol and its prisoners, and other duties such as the delivery of royal writs and the collection of taxes. The sheriff's office was burdensome and expensive and, although it was of annual duration only, many of the gentry were reluctant to serve. This was largely because the fees of the office could be reckoned in pence, whereas the expenses often came to hundreds of pounds.

The lord lieutenant

The office of lord lieutenant, a Tudor innovation, was initially created to deal with local emergencies in the dangers of the Reformation years. The lords lieutenants took on a more vigorous role, however, in the years before and after the Spanish Armada as they began to take over some of the sheriff's responsibilities. The lords lieutenants were normally peers of the realm and privy councillors, such as the Lords Cobham for Kent and Sussex and the earls of Derby for Lancashire and Cheshire. The office became continuous and their duties became more than military. This was because they became responsible for the collection of loans raised by the crown to meet extraordinary expenditure, for the supervision of recusants in their shires, and for the enforcement of orders from the privy council. These included such tasks as organising supplies for the navy and for military expeditions overseas, and seeing that grain was fairly distributed in times of scarcity. By the final years of Elizabeth's reign, the lords lieutenants and their deputies stood at the apex of country administration, but under the direct and constant supervision of the privy council. In this way, the lord lieutenant represented the crown and became the important link between central and local government. In centralising her control of the shires the creation of lieutenants was the queen's notable achievement in local government. However, local administration would have been impossible without the daily work of the justices of the peace, the constables of the hundreds and the parish officials. The shire was not the sole unit of local government; its sub-divisions were variously named, for example ridings in Yorkshire, lathes in Kent and rapes in Sussex. The parishes, as well as being ecclesiastical sub-divisions of the dioceses, also became units of civil jurisdiction and government. Many parish councils today retain some civil roles, for example providing polling stations during elections.

The justice of the peace

The justice of the peace was of early medieval origin, but by Elizabeth's reign there was a great increase in the numbers and work of the justices. In early Tudor England, there were, on average, less than ten justices to the shire but by the middle of Elizabeth's reign that average was about 40 or 50. In 1580, for example, their numbers had grown to 1,738 in total, the smallest number in any county being in Rutland where there were 13 and the largest in Kent where there were 83.

The increase in their work can be gauged from the growing number of parliamentary statutes that required the justice's assistance to make them work. William Lambarde in his celebrated *Eirenarcha* – the 1599 edition on the office of justice – reckoned the justice of the peace had to operate 306 such statutes; 38 of them were passed in the reigns of Edward VI and Mary and 75 in Elizabeth's reign between 1559 and 1597. Many of the latter dealt with such important and complex provisions such as apprenticeships, the poor and vagrancy, the famous social legislation of the reign which imposed heavy duties on the justices. The various acts, especially those of 1598 and 1601 which were the basis of the Elizabethan Poor Law for a system of poor relief, were not in fact superseded until the passing of the Poor Law Amendment Act of 1834.

The other source of the justice's powers and duties apart from parliament was the commission of the peace, which was the judicial side of the office as opposed to the administrative. The commission, dating back to the Middle Ages, was completely revised in 1590 and remained in force for three centuries. In brief, the commission authorised the justices to enforce all statutes concerning the peace; it gave them power to inquire by sworn inquest into all offences against the law and to hear and determine the outcome of a variety of cases and finally to hold regular sessions for their work. In that way, the justice had extensive criminal jurisdiction; he could commit culprits to gaol, and he could order the sheriff and bailiffs to search for thieves and robbers, punish riots, bail prisoners, convict for offences under the game laws, and deal with those who defaulted in paying their subsidies. Under the religious legislation of Elizabeth's reign, a justice could fine for non-attendance at church and report recusants to the privy council. Their administrative duties under the Poor Law were onerous: the appointment of overseers, the assessment of poor relief rates and the licensing of alehouses are a few examples.

The queen and privy council exercised control over the justices of the peace, but, since they were unpaid, the crown had to rely on their voluntary co-operation to enforce its will in the shires. The queen took a direct interest in their work and had no hesitation in ordering the removal of any justice of the peace who displeased her. Nor could the justices ignore the privy council, for from it poured out a stream of commands which became a flood by the 1590s.

The purpose of local government

The chief aims of the queen and her ministers in local government and administration were to maintain law and order in the country, to defend it against foreign invasion, and to raise sufficient money to ensure that the nation was protected and government carried out. Moreover, though less of a priority in the sixteenth century, local government also aimed to take a paternalistic interest in the welfare of its citizens. Yet the development of the Poor Law showed an increasing concern for the genuinely poor and unfortunate, as well as a determination to punish the sturdy rogues and wandering vagabonds. But punishments reflected a brutal age in their harshness as well as the power and ruthlessness of the justices; the stocks was the mildest penalty, flogging was frequent, and some offenders were sent to the galleys. Hanging was common-place – for example, in Derbyshire in the winter sessions of 1598, 18 criminals were hanged out of 65 tried, and in the spring sessions 12 out of 45.

The range and importance of the responsibilities, duties and powers of the local officials from the lord lieutenant down to the justice of the peace were in

A sturdy beggar being whipped through the streets by a constable. What was the attitude of local government officials both towards the genuinely poor and to rogues and vagabonds at this time?

effect the local application of the monarch's own power. The wearer of the crown possessed the fullness of authority and power. Sir Thomas Smith, in his *De republica Anglorum* (The commonweal of England), listed among the monarch's powers the sole right to make war and peace, to choose the privy council, to decide on foreign affairs, to invoke martial law, to fix and alter the currency, to grant pardons and dispensations from the laws and to fill all the chief offices in church and state: 'To be short, the prince is the life, the head and the authoritie of all thinges that be doone in the realme of England.'[14]

The cult of Gloriana and the Elizabethan Age

After the triumph over the Armada, Elizabeth I had become enshrined in the myths of the Virgin Queen and Gloriana, as the symbol and epitome of England's greatness. And ever since Camden's adulatory account of the queen, in his life of the queen and the annals of her reign, others have further embellished the picture. As a result, most biographers and historians assessing the reign find it difficult to appreciate the real historical personage of Elizabeth Tudor.

In the making of the cult, images and presentation were as important as the policies and the patronage. Elizabeth certainly capitalised on all the qualities commonly attributed to her sex. However, in W. T. MacCaffrey's view, 'Elizabeth's singular role as the royal actress was cast in a part written for a man.'[15] Nevertheless, as a Tudor ruler, she was as kingly as any of her predecessors, in, for example, the celebrated Tilbury speech, and ruled as well as reigned.[16] The queen was admired, flattered and idealised, and she revelled in the attention, encouraging those who had musical or literary talents to use them at her court and in her honour. Edmund Spenser, for example, a struggling private secretary until he produced his masterpiece, *The faerie queen*, remained in the shadows until Ralegh presented his work to the queen.

It was the great age of portrait painting; anyone of note, courtier, peer, merchant, and above all the queen herself, had portraits painted by such artists as William Larkin, George Gower, Nicholas Hilliard and Isaac Oliver. They did not paint true to life, 'warts and all', since the aim was to convey the wealth, splendour, the idealised noble qualities and worldly success of their great patrons. During the English Renaissance, those in positions of power and influence were often educated classicists and appreciative of the arts; men of the quality of Sir Philip Sidney, who was a poet, soldier and a hero. The queen's motto *Semper eadem* (Always the same) was difficult to achieve in portraiture as she waged a constant war to halt or evade the inevitable results of change and decay. Roy Strong has shown how unsuccessful attempts had been made to produce a single pattern portrait of Elizabeth so that her subjects could see one changeless and ageless countenance.[17] This deeply rooted conservatism can be traced in so many aspects of the reign: her fears of foreign wars, domestic disorders, above all treason and rebellion, her long attachments to favoured ministers and courtiers, and the stirrings of religious extremists, all reflected her psychological makeup and naturally affected the conduct of her statesmanship. A glance at her portraits will also reveal how heavy they are with the symbols of greatness.

The court was the natural setting of the cult of Gloriana with its round of conspicuous displays in the service of the queen: religious ceremonies, dances, masques, hunting and notably tilting, the mock combats that combined pageantry and literary games in which the jouster could display his wit. These were standard entertainment in all the royal palaces, but behind all the apparent trivialities there was a serious purpose – to show ardent loyalty to the principle of sovereignty itself, as well as to stimulate loyalty to the person of the queen in the court and at council.

The queen was also always anxious to reach out to the nation at large, hence the royal progresses centred on the great country houses, and the visits to town corporations. Here, despite the consequent impoverishment of members of the country elite that a royal visit entailed, there was always hope of patronage and possible appointments which lay in the crown's gift. These included pensions, annuities, monopolies, leases, titles and honours. These progresses, although, to some, mixed blessings, took place in the summer and were especially frequent in the 1570s and 1590s. Each lasted up to two months and covered hundreds of kilometres. The queen must have sat through hundreds of dramatic displays, musical entertainments and loyal addresses in which clerics polished up their latinity. As public relations exercises they were effective, for Elizabeth appreci- ated that monarchy was largely a matter of communication with the common people as much as with the courtiers. And in her last appearance before her

Queen Elizabeth I being carried in procession by her courtiers. The artist was probably Robert Peake (*fl.* 1580–1626). This picture was painted around 1600, but shows the queen as a more youthful figure. Ahead of the queen, are the Garter knights: Edmund Sheffield; Charles Howard of Effingham; George Clifford, duke of Cumberland; Thomas Butler, earl of Ormonde; an unknown courtier; George Talbot, earl of Shrewsbury and Edward Somerset, earl of Worcester.

'faithful Commons', her charm was still evident in the 'golden speech': 'Though God hath raised me high, yet this I account the glory of my crown, that I have reigned with your loves . . . by looking into the course by which I have ever holden since I began to reign . . . you may more easily discern in what kind of sympathy my care to benefit hath corresponded with your inclination to obey.'[18]

In general, most assessments of the queen's personality – and nearly all the facts about her have been discovered since the end of the nineteenth century – agree that she was mistress of her court and council and ruler of the realm and knew how to win the affection and command the obedience of most of her subjects. But how far the undoubted greatness of the Elizabethan Age, in its welter of poets, writers and playwrights, can be identified with the personality of Elizabeth Tudor is a controversial question. It is certainly true that many contemporaries equated the name and fame of the monarch with the emergent English nation.[19] Unquestionably, too, there is more to the successes of Elizabethan England than the leadership of the queen alone. When people looked back from the seventeenth century, the days of 'Good Queen Bess', 'The Virgin Queen' and 'Gloriana' looked like a golden age when Englishmen first became aware of themselves as a nation, conscious of their achievements, traditions and potential.

However, England in 1603 still had its unresolved constitutional problems. It also had grave economic difficulties, for at least 40 per cent of its population lived at or under subsistence level. Ireland, 'Spain's postern gate', though reconquered under Lord Mountjoy, remained unpacified. How secure and how united was the heritage which Elizabeth passed on to James I? Although England was spared the horrors of war at home and had staved off the threat of foreign invasion, this achievement was won at great cost. The queen's subjects had suffered unrelieved taxation for over two decades, so that, at the end, instead of ending in a blaze of glory, the Elizabethan age ended for many in despair and disillusionment.

Document case study

Elizabeth I, 1588–1603

8.1 Provisions for the protection of the queen in the event of invasion

*A note about the footsoldiers needed, for 'The guard of Her Majesty's person',
June 1588. This is from Sir Thomas Scott, deputy lieutenant of Kent, belatedly
answering a privy council letter demanding that 2,000 of the best footsoldiers in
Kent should be sent to London to guard the queen's person, if the necessity
arose*

Whereas by occasion Sir John Norris and ourselves were much busied yesterday in viewing marshalling and training of the most part of the select and trained bands of this county of Kent . . . it was not remembered to answer a letter of the Lords of the Council a good time since concerning the sending forth 2000 out of the county to attend Her

Majesty's person and 4000 to make head against the enemy after he is landed . . . we think it meet that out of the number of 2500 trained soldiers, 200 of the best be sent to attend Her Majesty and 500 of the worst . . . left to join with the other bands to the 4000 we verily think may be sent to make head as aforseaid.

Source: *State papers domestic*, Elizabeth, vol. 211/89

8.2 Elizabeth's reaction to the threat of invasion

From the queen's Tilbury speech to her troops in August 1588

My loving people, we have been persuaded by some that are careful of our safety to take heed how we commit ourselves to armed multitudes for fear of treachery. Let tyrants fear. I have always so behaved myself that, under God, I have placed my chiefest strength and safeguard in the loyal hearts and goodwill of my subjects. And therefore I am come amongst you, as you see at this time, not for my recreation and disport, but being resolved, in the midst and heat of the battle, to live or die amongst you all; to lay down for my God and for my kingdom and for my people, my honour and my blood even in the dust. I know that I have the body of a weak and feeble woman, but I have the heart and stomach of a king, and a king of England too! And think foul scorn that Parma or Spain, or any prince of Europe, should dare to invade the borders of my realm . . . I myself will take up arms, I myself will be your general, judge and rewarder of every one of your virtues in the field.

Source: G. Mattingley, *The Armada*, London, 1959, p. 350

8.3 A Spaniard's account of his reception in Ireland

From Captain Don Francisco Cuellar's account of the Spanish Armada and his adventures in Connaught and Ulster, AD 1589. His ship was wrecked on the Sligo coast after the rout of the Armada

These people call themselves Christians. Mass is said among them and regulated according to the orders of the church of Rome. The majority of their churches, monasteries and hermitages have been demolished by the hands of the English who are in garrison . . . in this kingdom there is neither justice nor right . . . from the thirteen ships of our Armada in which came so many people of importance, all of whom were drowned, these savages obtained much riches in jewellery and money and word of this reached the great Governor of the Queen in Dublin and he went with seventeen hundred soldiers to search for the lost ships and the people who had escaped . . . my chief cause of misery was that I had no means of embarking for the Kingdom of Scotland until I heard of the territory of Prince Ocan [O'Cahan or O'Kane] where there were some vessels going to Scotland . . . he had twelve Spaniards with him to pass over to Scotland and was much delighted with my arrival especially when the soldiers told him I was a captain.

Source: Captain Don Francisco Cuellar, *Captain Cuellar's narrative of the Spanish Armada and his adventures in Connaught and Ulster, AD 1589*, ed. and tr. R. Crawford, London, 1897

8.4 The need for extra subsidies to continue the war

Sir Thomas Egerton, the Lord Keeper of the Great Seal, in a speech to parliament, 1597

[which] was fought not as previous wars had been . . . either of ambition to enlarge dominions, or of revenge to quit injuries but because the holy religion of God is sought to be rooted out, the whole realm to be subdued, and the precious life of her excellent Majesty to be taken away . . . (she) had not spared to disburse a mass of treasure and to sell her land for maintenance of her armies by sea and land (therefore contributions were essential) . . . He that would seek to lay up treasure and so enrich himself, should be like to him that would busy himself to beautify his house when the city where he dwelleth were on fire, or to deck up his cabin when the ship wherein he saileth were ready to drown . . . to give is to give to ourselves.

[In the same parliament Sir Robert Cecil added] In Ireland we have an army and nothing but an army; fed, even, out of England.

Source: J. E. Neale, *Elizabeth and her parliaments: 1584–1601*, London, 1957, ch. 5

8.5 A contemporary view of Elizabeth

From John Clapham's Certain Observations concerning the life and reign of Queen Elizabeth, *1603. Clapham belonged to Burghley's household in the last years of that statesman's life*

She was of nature somewhat hasty but quickly appeased . . . her greatest griefs of mind and body she either patiently endured or politely dissembled . . . she would often show herself abroad at public spectacles even against her own liking so that the people might perceive her ability of body and good disposition which otherwise in respect of her years they might have perhaps have doubted; so jealous was she to have her natural defects discovered for diminishing her reputation.

Source: E. P. and C. Read (eds.), J. Clapham, *Elizabeth of England*, Philadelphia, 1951, pp. 89–90

8.6 A contemporary view on the reasons for the increase in population

From a speech made in 1594 by William Lambarde to the commission of the peace in Kent. Lambarde was an antiquarian, a historian of Kent and Keeper of the Records in the Tower

That the number of our people is multiplied, it is both demonstrable to the eye and evident in reason, considering that on the one side nowadays not only young folk of all sorts but churchmen also of each degree do marry and multiply at liberty, which was not wont to be, and on the other side, that we have not, God be thanked, been touched with any extreme mortality, either by sword or sickness that might abate the overgrown number of us.

Source: Lambarde to the justices at Maidstone, 17 January 1594, from C. Read (ed.), *William Lambarde and local government*, New York, p. 182

Document case-study questions

1 What evidence does 8.1 provide of preparation for possible Spanish invasion in 1588?

2 Elizabeth's speech to her troops at Tilbury in August 1588 in 8.2 was designed to raise spirits and also to assert her rights as monarch. How does the language used in the speech allow her to achieve this?

3 What evidence for the state of religion and government in Ireland can be obtained from 8.3? In what respects can the document be said to be biased?

4 In 8.4, how effectively does Sir Thomas Egerton make the case for extra subsidies to continue the war?

5 In what ways does 8.5 show why Elizabeth was a largely successful monarch?

6 What, according to 8.6, was the cause of 'distress' in the 1590s?

Notes and references

1 There is a multitude of narrative accounts of the defeat of the Armada; perhaps still one of the best is G. Mattingley, *The defeat of the Spanish Armada*, London, 1959; and the May 1988 commemorative issue of *History today* is full of illustrative material and fresh insights. For the lesser known civil defence preparations see this author's 'Armada preparations in Kent' in *Archaeologia Cantiana*, 85, (1970).

2 For this last point see L. Boynton, *The Elizabethan militia*, London, 1967.

3 J. Thirsk, *The agrarian history of England and Wales, 1500–1640*, vol. 4, London, 1976; and A. B. Appleby, *Famine in Tudor and Stuart England*, Liverpool, 1978.

4 J. U. Neff, *The rise of the British coal industry*, vols. 1 and 2, London, 1932; and A. Simpson, *The wealth of the gentry*, Chicago, 1961; and for an overview, P. Ramsey, *Tudor economic problems*, London, 1966; and J. Hatcher, *The history of the British coal industry*, vol. 1, Oxford 1998.

5 See below, Note 6, and John McGurk, *The Elizabethan conquest of Ireland: the 1590's crisis*, Manchester, 1997.

6 J. E. Neale, *Elizabeth I and her parliaments 1584–1601*, vol. 2, London, 1957, pp. 280–310.

7 The queen had the power of veto which she used on 67 occasions, an average of five vetoes in each of her parliaments. She also did not hesitate to imprison very difficult members of parliament such as Peter Wentworth, Anthony Cope, Edward Lewkenor, Ranulf Hurleston and Robert Bainbridge, all of whom spent remaining sessions of parliament in the Tower. See Neale, *Elizabeth I and her parliaments*.

8 We know less about the House of Lords in the period partly because the Elizabethan peers did not keep parliamentary diaries, but they were more subservient to the crown than the Lower House. That is why bills likely to meet with much opposition in the Lower House were often introduced in the Lords; see, for example, W. Notestein, 'The winning of the initiative by the House of Commons', British Academy, Ralegh lecture in history, 1924.

9 This was the occasion on which the queen graciously retracted and promised reform in the matter of monopolies.

10 See, for example, John McGurk, 'Welfare measures of the sick and wounded of the Nine Years' War in Ireland' in *Journal of the society for army historical research*, vol. 68 (spring and autumn 1990).

11 Whereas, in the period from 1559 to 1589 the demand was for a total of nine subsidies over the 30-year period.

12 H. Townshend, *Historical collections, 1680*, pp. 178–179.

13 Simon Adams, 'Faction, clientage and party-English politics 1550–1603', in *History today* (December 1982).

14 Sir Thomas Smith, *De republica Anglorum*, revised edn, 1570, p. 62; and M. Dewar, *Sir Thomas Smith: a Tudor intellectual in office*, London, 1964.

15 W. T. MacCaffrey, *Elizabeth I: war and politics 1588–1603*, Princeton, 1992, p. 542. See also the Select bibliography under Elizabeth.

16 See document 8.2 in this chapter.

17 R. Strong, *Gloriana: the portraits of Queen Elizabeth I*, 1987, p. 12.

18 Neale, *Elizabeth I and her parliaments*, pp. 393 ff.

19 In the literature of the age, not only in the political speeches and puritan pamphlets, but also from the pens of the great, like Shakespeare, Ralegh and Spenser, there is much frank political and social criticism.

Conclusion

Over the last thirty years, historians have revised former interpretations of the fifteenth and sixteenth centuries. Detailed research in official government records, both national and local, and in all manner of institutional and family histories has changed our views of these two centuries. A few of the major aspects of historical revisionism on the theme of monarchy in the British Isles are discussed here.

The Wars of the Roses

J. R. Lander, for example, has shown that the period of the Wars of the Roses was not one of total confusion or of continual warring between factions. He argued that the amount of fighting was small, estimating that there was only about thirteen weeks of actual conflict over 32 years. He concluded, therefore, that these wars had a small effect on the population at large. So, instead of viewing the fifteenth century as one of barbarism, Lander sees the English peasants rising in prosperity to a level that they would not experience again until the eighteenth century.

It is also now commonplace to regard the reigns of Edward IV and of Henry VII as being similar in aim and methods. And, although the house of York fell in 1485 and the Tudor dynasty was established, the year 1485 is no longer considered to be the beginning of a 'modern era'.

Historical revisionism is of course a living debate. New sources are discovered, interpretations are refined, and new emphases and insights are found that change traditional views. Recent evaluations, for example, of Edward IV by C. Ross, his most recent biographer, claims that Edward's reputation has risen too high in comparison with that of Henry VI. And, in Ross's view, Edward IV was not as clever, ruthless or as consistent as Henry VII. A. J. Pollard maintains that other historians have put too great an emphasis on the points of continuity between the fifteenth and sixteenth centuries in the personal government of the monarch.[1] Pollard argues that the monarchy was at its weakest between 1450 and 1480 more than at any time since Edward the Confessor (d. 1066), and that, in that period, Henry VI, Edward V and Richard III all lost the throne and also that Edward IV was temporarily dethroned. Again, Henry VII's great achievement was to have survived a series of rebellions, to have restored the monarchy to stability and to have left government strong and solvent after disorder in the realm. It is worth considering, however, whether this achievement was due to the fact that Henry's council in work and composition was almost identical to that of his Yorkist predecessors (more than half the Yorkist councillors still alive in 1485 were used by Henry VII) and in what sense, therefore, 1485 was indeed a watershed in the history of the monarchy.

Overmighty subjects

There is also a continuing debate on 'bastard feudalism' – a term commonly used to describe the increasing power and influence of the nobility, with their liveried retainers and private armies who were loyal to their lords and not to the crown. K. B. MacFarlane spent much effort rejecting that interpretation, arguing instead that the retainers were for the use of the nobility in peacetime not in war, and that, instead of promoting disorder, they made stable administration possible in the shires. P. Williams would also support that view, observing that the body of retainers in the noble households were an essential ingredient in the way of life of the late medieval period.

M. Hicks, on the other hand, would argue that Richard III, for example, was more powerful as the duke of Gloucester than as a monarch. He was, after all, duke for much longer, subduing his great rivals, Warwick, Clarence, Northumberland, Somerset, Hastings and the Woodvilles. Some modern historians also revert to earlier views that the root cause of the Wars of the Roses was the increasing power and influence of the great nobility.

It is still debatable, therefore, whether the overmighty subject or the weak monarch was the more significant cause of political and social chaos between 1450 and 1485. The influence of chance and the accidental can never be underestimated. An Italian observing affairs in England in the year 1500 wrote:

> This kingdom has been for the last 600 years governed by one king, who is not elected but succeeds by hereditary right. Should there be no direct heir, and the succession be disputed, the question is often settled by force of arms . . . and, therefore, it has been an understood thing that he who lost the day lost the kingdom also.[2]

Moreover, monarchical rule varied with the personalities of the rulers and how their decisions were made. Were they made arbitrarily or by persuasion of their advisers, or forced on them by council or by parliament, or made hastily in reaction to crises rather than according to doctrinaire books of law or constitutions? Examples of all these varieties of the exercise of political power can be found under the Tudor monarchs.

Parliament

The whole question of parliament is a thorny one and easy to misinterpret, especially in the sixteenth century. It was an important institution of government, but very different from today's parliament. Its role was one of partnership with the monarch, not an official opposition to the ruler. The day-to-day work of government was not parliament's but the king's and his council's; it must be stressed that the dominant governmental institution remained the crown and, for most of the time, it ruled without parliament. The monarch summoned parliament. Henry VII, for example, called but seven parliaments in his reign of 24 years and Elizabeth I called a total of ten parliaments during a reign of 45 years. Parliaments were called to make laws, to grant taxes and for general consultation. The rise of the House of Commons at the expense of the Lords and the king was not a feature of Tudor government. The whole subject of the rise of parliament is an epic one but belongs to the nineteenth and twentieth centuries.

Tudor despotism?

The view that there was a Tudor despotism characteristic of the whole dynasty held the field for many centuries. A. F. Pollard in the 1920s and J. E. Neale in the 1950s, however, argued strongly that the House of Commons made significant progress in the reign of Elizabeth, inspired mainly by puritan opposition to the crown.

However, in the 1970s and 1980s, G. R. Elton and his 'disciples' attacked Neale's arguments and use of evidence, to convince other historians that the Elizabethan House of Commons did not even attempt to act as an opposition to the crown, nor did it rise in prominence at the crown's expense. They argued that, instead, there is enough evidence on the contrary to show that it entered a period of decline.

Neale's critics, however, do not go so far as to conclude that there was a Tudor despotism after all. Co-operation with the crown for the sake of good government was the purpose and aim of most members of the Elizabethan parliaments. However, it is also true to state that many of the root causes of the Stuart kings' conflict with parliament in the next century can be traced back to the tensions in government in the last decades of Elizabeth's reign. It should be noted, too, that in Elton's many books and articles, referred to throughout this book, he maintained that there had been a revolution in government under Thomas Cromwell. He argues that Thomas Cromwell aimed to take much of the administration out of the royal household and vest it in a number of bureaucratic institutions. In particular, in taking the office of the King's Secretary out of the royal household and giving it a new important status as one of the great offices of state, he exploited its intimacy with the king for his own ends. The thesis has generated much criticism, especially on the role and character that Elton gives Thomas Cromwell as innovator and statesman. Was there a Tudor revolution in government? Was Cromwell an innovator in policy making or did he simply carry out his master's wishes with ruthless efficiency? These questions are still live issues among historians.

The centralisation of authority

In discussing the theme of monarchy, we have been confronted with the problems facing monarchs in their efforts to centralise their authority. As far as unifying the British Isles is concerned, it would be too simplistic to say that Tudor monarchs followed a relentlessly uniform policy. Although there were so-called Acts of Union with Wales in 1536 and 1543, assimilating Welsh government to the English, and Ireland had been made a sister kingdom under the English crown in 1541, constitutional unity within these islands did not take place until the Act of Union with Scotland in 1707. The union of 1603 was the union of two crowns heralding the new dynasty of the Stuarts – and the Act of Union with Ireland was not passed until 1801. If they had a common policy, which is never called 'foreign policy' with respect to the British Isles, the Tudors certainly wished to extend their authority by means of alliances, political or dynastic, and by military coercion when they could afford it. This was because, in the interests of the defence of the realm of England, they wished to prevent Ireland, Scotland or Wales from being used by continental enemies as back doors by which they could attack England.

As the Tudor monarchs went about the centralisation of their government and administration, they were hampered by the ever present communication difficulties caused by geography and language. London was the centre of government. Royal progresses never went outside England; indeed, Elizabeth I ventured little further north than Warwickshire. Maps, where they existed, were inaccurate and crude. Christopher Saxton was still mapping the shires of England in the late 1570s. The problems, moreover, that the different languages of the British Isles presented to government officials appears to have been underestimated (and under-studied). Although Latin was used as a *lingua franca* in many negotiations, in Wales, Ireland and Scotland much must have depended on the reliability and truthfulness of the interpreters.

The monarch and council always had to depend on their local representatives to interpret their will throughout the realm. This is the reason for the elaborate system of lords lieutenants, their deputies, the justices of the peace, the sheriffs and, down through the hierarchical structure of local government, to the humblest constables of the hundreds and to the churchwardens in the parishes. Naturally, the system seems to have worked best in the shires nearest to the seat of government. The monarchs had no standing army. The shire militias and the trained bands were for defence, and from time to time expeditionary forces were raised (and the trained bands raided) to fight outside England.

By means of the Council in the Marches of Wales and in the Council of the North, the Tudors tried to maintain law and order and to curb the powers of the old nobility. But many, like the Dacres, the Derbys, the Percys and the Fitzgeralds, retained some vestiges of their ancient privileges and could exercise more influence than royal officials. It is interesting to note that it was not until Elizabeth's reign that the earls of Derby, for instance, relinquished their title as 'Kings of the Isle of Man'. Did the north of England prolong feudal-type relations longer than elsewhere? Furthermore, the north of England, predominantly Catholic, posed increased dangers for the government in the age of the Reformation. Political turbulence in the North quietened as the Council of the North became more active and vigorous, which it did during its suppression of the serious rebellion of 1569.

Historical interpretation and Elizabeth's reign, 1588–1603

There are varying interpretations of the second half of Elizabeth's reign. The aftermath of the Armada marks a watershed to some historians but not all. To some historians, the victory over the Armada of 1588 marked the peak of England's power and the decline of Spain as an imperial power, yet the war continued long after 1588; the subsequent victories in the destruction of Cadiz in 1596 and Mountjoy's defeat of the combined Spanish and Irish forces at Kinsale in 1601 still did not end the conflict with Spain. This went into the next reign and did not end until peace was made by James VI, now James I of England, in 1604. In Europe, the Netherlands continued to be the chief theatre of war in the Dutch struggle for independence.

In political and constitutional history, the successors of A. F. Pollard's interpretation, such as S. T. Bindoff and J. E. Neale, have also seen the years from 1588 to 1603 as foreshadowing the great constitutional struggles between the crown and parliament, which were a distinctive aspect of the seventeenth century. G. R. Elton emphasised the continuity of these years with the earlier part of Elizabeth's reign, claiming that 1588, the *annus mirabilis*, has been exaggerated by historians overimpressed with hindsight.

We have also seen how Tudor policy, or lack of it, towards Ireland was complex and inconsistent. Should Ireland be treated, for example, as a lordship, a kingdom, or a colony? Under Henry VII, war and conspiracy meant that intervention was necessary and that royal rights had to be asserted. Henry VIII tried to continue the policy of aristocratic delegation, the cheapest way to run Ireland, with the Fitzgeralds as his representative. Later, he experimented with an Anglicising policy. This involved the practice of 'Surrender and Re-grant' and the constitutional device of making Ireland a kingdom under the crown of England. At one stage, he planned that his illegitimate son, Henry Fitzroy, should be crowned king of Ireland.

Under Elizabeth, until the last decade of the reign, a pattern of intermittent violence, rather than all-out conquest, followed by attempts at peaceful persuasion may be detected in the careers of the many Lords Deputy of Ireland. But their effective authority is centred largely in Dublin and the Pale. W. T. MacCaffrey considers that the Irish Elizabethan conquest 'was the one great success of Elizabeth's arms and the most disastrous failure of Elizabethan policy making'.[3] Fundamental issues remained unresolved: a discontented Old English aristocracy, a resurgent Gaelic populace and, among the New English, an underpaid coterie of officials, not to mention an unpaid soldiery, all hungry for rewards. Did Ireland then become a welcome legacy to James VI and I for, after Elizabeth's victory, Ulster lands were to become fair game for confiscation and plantation in the seventeenth century? On the other hand, were the difficulties of ruling Ireland to be made worse by the policy of plantation?

Tudor policy towards Scotland become complicated by the Reformation and the 'Auld Alliance' with France. Henry VII's marriage policy brought a period of peace, and it ultimately led to the union of the crowns in the person of the son of

Mary Queen of Scots, James VI of Scotland, I of England, Wales and Ireland. Henry VIII, and the duke of Somerset after him, tried for a closer union of the two countries by proposing a further dynastic marriage of the young Edward to King James V's daughter Mary. But by her subsequent marriage with the dauphin, the future King Francis II, the Franco-Scottish alliance was cemented, particularly as Mary's mother, Mary of Guise, became regent to rule Scotland. Mary's claim to the English throne was indisputable as a direct descendant of Henry VII and also as a Catholic. Mary became a threat and a focus of plots for Elizabeth's enemies. But it was only after Mary had been in England for 20 years that Elizabeth agreed to Mary's execution in 1587. Many historians have remarked upon the docility of James VI to the execution of his mother, for he seems to have gone out of his way to placate Elizabeth, doubtless in anticipation of succeeding to her throne. In Jenny Wormald's judgement, '1603 resolved one thing and one thing only for Tudor Englishmen and Stewart Scotsmen. The English acquired a successor to Elizabeth. The Scots lost a full-time king. Beyond that lay nothing but confusion and muddle.'[4]

Many interesting questions remain concerning the Tudor monarchies. Why were there so many rebellions during the Tudor century? Why, in fact, did the Tudor dynasty survive? How successful were these monarchs in centralising government and administration? Why was there no major revolt in the 1590s? And why do twentieth-century historians hold different views of the Tudors – their lives, motives and policies over the Tudor period from 1485 to 1603?

Notes and references

1 A. J. Pollard, *The Wars of the Roses*, London, 1983.

2 C. A. Syned (ed.), *A relation of the island of England*, Camden Society, 1847, p. 46.

3 W. T. MacCaffrey, *Elizabeth I: war and politics, 1588–1603*, Princeton, 1992, p. 572.

4 J. Wormald, 'One king, two kingdoms', in A. Grant and K. J. Stringer (eds.), *Uniting the kingdom – the making of British history*, London, 1995, p. 123.

Select bibliography

The monarchy

See Sir John Fortescue, *On the laws and governance of England*, ed. and tr. by S. Lockwood, Cambridge, 1997. M. J. Wilks, *The problem of sovereignty in the later middle ages*, Cambridge, 1963, is heavily theoretical but important on sovereignty. Many aspects of court life are treated in D. Starkey (ed.), *The English court from the Wars of the Roses to the Civil War*, London, 1987. J. H. Burns, *The true law of kingship: concepts of monarchy in early modern Scotland*, Oxford, 1996; and J. Cannon and R. Griffiths (eds.), *The Oxford illustrated history of the British monarchy*, Oxford, 1995.

For an overview of the period, see D. M. Loades, *Politics and the nation, 1450–1660*, 3rd edn, Hassocks, 1986; and for government and politics before Henry VIII, see J. R. Lander, *Government and community: England 1450–1509*, London, 1977; and J. Guy, *Tudor England*, Oxford, 1990.

York and Lancaster: the background to the Tudors

For an overview of the history of England from 1461 to 1485, see D. M. Loades, *Politics and the Nation 1450–1660*, Part I, Hassocks, 3rd edn, 1986; and for the king in medieval political life, see J. Watts, *Henry VI and the politics of kingship*, Cambridge, 1997. For images of kingship, see P. Binski, *Westminster Abbey and the Plantagenets: kingship and the representation of power, 1200–1400*, London, 1995; A. Goodman, *The Wars of the Roses*, London, 1995; and D. Bentley-Cranch, *Royal faces*, London, 1990.

For the major personalities mentioned in this and the following chapters, see the Yale University Press paperback series, *English monarchs*, such as C. Ross, *Edward IV*, Yale, 1977; and his *Richard III*, Yale, 1981; and B. P. Wolffe's *Henry VI*, 1983. But for brief biographical notes on the monarchs, see C. Haigh (ed.), *The Cambridge historical encyclopedia of Great Britain and Ireland*, Cambridge, 1985; C. Given-Wilson, *An illustrated history of late-medieval England*, Manchester, 1996; and M. Magnusson (ed.), *Chambers biographical dictionary*, Edinburgh, 1990. J. Gillingham (ed.), 'Richard III, a medieval kingship', *History today*, London (1994), reviews many of the controversies. Also, see M. Hicks, *Richard III and his rivals: magnates and their motives in the Wars of the Roses*, London, 1997. There are many biographies of Thomas More but the most succinct can be found in A. Kenny, *Thomas More*, Oxford past masters series, Oxford, 1987.

For the importance of royal government in the provinces in this period, see P. Fleming, A. Gross and J. R. Lander (eds.), *Regionalism and revision: the crown and its provinces in England 1250–1650*, Hambledon, 1997, a set of essays which incorporate much recent research.

For the specific duties of the local justices of the peace, see J. R. Lander, *English justices of the peace, 1461–1509*, Cheltenham, 1989. For important insights into the pre-Reformation church in England, see M. Harvey, *England, Rome and the papacy, 1417–1464*, Manchester, 1993; R. N. Swanson, *Church and society in late medieval England*, Oxford, 1989; and C. Clough (ed.), *Profession, vocation and culture in later medieval England*, Liverpool, 1982.

Henry VII: 1485–1509

There is brief coverage of Henry VII's reign in G. R. Elton, *England under the Tudors*, London, 3rd edn, 1991; and in J. Guy, *Tudor England*, Oxford, 2nd edn, 1990. For contemporary evaluations of Henry VII and his times, see Polydore Vergil, *Anglica historia (1485–1537)*, ed. and tr. D. Hay, Camden Series, London, 1950; and likewise, the celebrated life by Francis Bacon, *History of the reign of Henry VII*, J. R. Lumby (ed.), Cambridge, 1885.

For historical controversy on Henry, see two essays by G. R. Elton in vol. 1 of his collected works: *Studies in Tudor and Stuart politics and government*, Cambridge, 1974. For more recent and briefer accounts, see A. Grant, *Henry VII*, Lancaster, 1985; C. Rogers, *Henry VII*, Access to history, 1991; and the revised edition of R. Lockyer, *Henry VII*, London, 1983.

On the challenges to Henry's throne from Ireland in the Lambert Simnel and Perkin Warbeck Rebellions, see M. Levine, *Tudor dynastic problems, 1460–1571*, London, 1973; J. R. Lander, *Government and community; England 1450–1509*, London, 1980; S. Ellis, *Tudor Ireland, 1470–1603*, London, 1985; and his *Tudor frontiers and noble power*, London, 1996. Much recent research has been collated in I. Arthurson, *The Perkin Warbeck conspiracy 1491–1499*, Cheltenham, 1994.

The importance of the House of Kildare in Ireland is well brought out in A. Cosgrove (ed.), *The new history of Ireland*, vol. 2, Dublin, 1980; and, likewise, for the importance of the great Percy family of Northumberland, see J. M. W. Bean, *The estates of the Percy family, 1416–1537*, Oxford, 1958.

Note that a recent work, G. Bernard, *The Tudor nobility*, Manchester, 1992, challenges some of the past assessments on political change under the Tudors.

For a survey of the church in pre-Reformation England, see R. N. Swanson, *Faith, religion and observance before the Reformation*, Manchester, 1996; and the same author's *Church and society in late medieval England*, Oxford, 1989.

For the history of Scotland, see J. Wormald (ed.), *Scotland revisited*, London, 1991.

Henry VIII: 1509–1547

There are scores of biographies of Henry VIII. The standard one is now the revised edition of J. J. Scarisbrick, *Henry VIII*, Yale, 1997. For a brief acute analysis, see G. R. Elton, *Henry VIII*, London, new edn, 1978; and D. Starkey, *The reign of Henry VIII: personalities and politics*, London, 1985. There is a recent and important synthesis in D. MacCulloch, *The reign of Henry VIII*, London, 1996. But for a collection of specialised articles, especially on government and the roles of Wolsey and Thomas Cromwell, see G. R. Elton, *Studies in Tudor and Stuart politics and government*, 4 vols., Cambridge, 1974–92. The relevant one for this chapter is Vol. 1, 1974. Elton's *The Tudor constitution*, Cambridge, 2nd edn, 1982, gives a collection of primary documentary sources. For essays in criticism of Elton, see C. Coleman and D. Starkey (eds.), *Revolution re-assessed*, Oxford, 1986. Less controversial is Elton's *Reform and Reformation: England 1509–1558*, London, 1977.

The Henrician or early Reformation in England has attracted an equally vast number of treatments and the latest are not always to be unreservedly recommended, but see H. M. Smith, *Henry VIII and the Reformation*, London, 1948; and A. G. Dickens, *The English Reformation*, London, 1965, a reprint of a new edition. For a convenient collection of documents on the Reformation, see A. G. Dickens and D. Carr (eds.), *The Reformation in England to the accession of Elizabeth II*, London, reprinted 1975. See also W. J. Shields, *The English Reformation 1530–1570*, London, 1989; E. Duffy, *The stripping of the altars*, Yale, 1994; C. Haigh, *Reformation and resistance in Tudor Lancashire*, Cambridge, 1975; M. Bush, *The Pilgrimage of Grace*, Manchester, 1996; and C. Cross, *Church and people 1450–1660: the triumph of the laity in the English church*, London, 1976, which has important documentary sources. Also see C. Haigh, *English Reformation*, Oxford, 1993.

For Wales, see G. Williams, *The Welsh church from conquest to Reformation*, Cardiff, 1976 and his *Wales, c. 1415–1642: recovery, re-orientation and reformation*, Oxford, 1987; and C. Brady, 'Comparable histories?: Tudor reform in Wales and Ireland', in S. Ellis and S. Barber (eds.), *Conquest and union: fashioning a British state 1485–1725*, London, 1995.

For Scotland, see M. Lynch, *Scotland: a new history*, 2nd edn, London, 1992.

For Ireland, see the chapters by D. B. Quinn and G. A. Hayes-McCoy in *The new history of Ireland*, vol. 3, Oxford, new edn, 1976; and the first two chapters in N. Canny, *From Reformation to Restoration: Ireland 1534–1660*, Dublin, 1987. For more detail on Anglicised Ireland, see S. Ellis, *Reform and revival: English government in Ireland 1470–1534*, London, 1986. The only work of importance on the dissolution of the monasteries in Ireland is that by Brendan Bradshaw, *The dissolution of the religious orders in Ireland under Henry VIII*, Cambridge, 1974. For an explanation of why the Reformation generally failed in Ireland, see Colm Lennon, *The lords of Dublin in the age of Reformation*, Dublin, 1989.

Edward VI: 1547–1553

The best accounts of the reign of Edward VI are D. Hoak, *The king's council in the reign of Edward VI*, Cambridge, 1976; and G. R. Elton, *Reform and Reformation*, London, 1977, which rehabilitates Northumberland and is critical of Somerset. For a fuller account of the latter, see M. Bush, *The government policy of Protector Somerset*, London, 1975. For Northumberland, see B. L. Beer, *Northumberland: the political career of John Dudley, earl of Warwick and duke of Northumberland*, Ohio, 1973. General overviews of the reign are given in J. Guy, *Tudor England*, Oxford, 1990; and P. Williams, *The later Tudors: England 1547–1603*, Oxford, 1995.

For a useful biography of Edward VI, see W. K. Jordan, *Edward VI: the young king*, London, 1968.

On the rebellions, see A. Fletcher, *Tudor rebellions*, 3rd edn, London, 1983, which has a good descriptive analysis of political unrest and a collection of sources. Specifically on the 1549 rebellion, see D. MacCulloch, 'Kett's Rebellion in context', *Past and present*, vol. 84 (1979).

Mary Tudor: 1553–1558

The modern authority on Mary Tudor and her reign is D. M. Loades, see *The reign of Mary Tudor: politics, government and religion in England, 1553–1558*, London, 1979; his life of the queen in *Mary Tudor*, Oxford, 1989; and *John Dudley, duke of Northumberland 1504–1553*, Oxford, 1996, a biography in which he discusses Northumberland's efforts to frustrate Mary's claim to the throne. The Spanish marriage and its problems are also covered by Loades in 'Philip II and the government of England', in C. Cross *et al* (eds.), *Law and government under the Tudors*, Cambridge, 1988. But also see Chapter 17 in G. R. Elton, *Reform and Reformation*, London, 1977; and J. Loach, *Parliament and the crown in the reign of Mary Tudor*, Oxford, 1986.

For a composite study of the Marian martyrs, see D. M. Loades, *The Oxford martyrs*, London, 1970.

For the rebellion of Thomas Wyatt, see A. Fletcher, *Tudor rebellions*, 3rd edn, London, 1983; and M. R. Thorp, 'Religion and the Wyatt Rebellion of 1554', in *Church history*, vol. 47 (1978). See also the essays on Mary's reign in F. Heal and R. O'Day, *Church and society in England: Henry VIII to James I*, London, 1977; and by the same authors, *The debate on the English Reformation*, London, 1995.

Elizabeth I: the early years, 1558–1588

This is a highly selective list; there are, for instance, over seventy biographies of Elizabeth published in the last century. Authoritative works listed here carry their own bibliographies and from them you will be aware of changing interpretations of the history of Elizabeth's long reign. For one bibliographical review, see C. Haigh, 'The reign of Elizabeth', in *History today* (1985), in the feature 'The reading of history'; J. P. Keynon, 'Queen Elizabeth and the historians', in S. Adams (ed.), *Queen Elizabeth: most politik princess*, London, 1984, will also help towards an understanding of the varying interpretations of the reign. William Camden could be called Elizabeth's official historian and his version of events has greatly dominated Elizabethan history; on this aspect, see John McGurk, 'William Camden: civil historian or Gloriana's propagandist', in *History today* (1988).

On political and religious developments, W. T. MacCaffrey's trilogy provides an up-to-date narrative: *The shaping of the Elizabethan regime; Elizabethan politics 1558–1572*, London, 1969; *Queen Elizabeth and the making of policy, 1572–1588*, Princeton, 1981; and *Elizabeth I: war and politics, 1588–1603*, Princeton, 1992. MacCaffrey's last named title and the recent biography of the queen, *Elizabeth I*, London, 1993, takes much recent research into account. C. Haigh (ed.), *The reign of Elizabeth*, London, reprinted 1985, is a collection of essays also incorporating research. But J. Guy, *Tudor England*, London, 1990, supersedes some of the older narratives. Note also, J. Guy (ed.), *The reign of Elizabeth: court and culture in the last decade*, Cambridge, 1995.

In P. Collinson's classic account of puritanism, *The Elizabethan puritan movement*, London, new edn, 1990, he plays down the puritan opposition to Elizabeth. See also his *The religion of Protestants*, Oxford, 1982. Recent work on the history of Catholicism shows it to be less militant but more widespread in the reign. For a brief analysis and collection of documents on this theme, see A. Dures, *English Catholicism 1558–1642*, London, 1983; but the work of D. MacCulloch on late English Reformation studies is now becoming important, see *Suffolk and the Tudors*, Oxford, 1986; and his *The later Reformation in England 1547–1603*, London, 1990.

On parliament, see J. E. Neale's two volumes, *Elizabeth and her parliaments: 1559–1581*, London, 1953 and *Elizabeth and her parliaments: 1584–1601*, London, 1957. These have been much challenged by G. R. Elton. See particularly, his collected essays and papers in *Studies in Tudor and Stuart politics and government*, vol. 3, Cambridge, 1983; and more recently in his *The parliament of England 1559–1581*, Cambridge, 1986. But for an introduction to the whole theme of Elizabeth's parliaments, see J. Loach, *Parliament under the Tudors*, Oxford, 1991; M. R. Graves, *Elizabethan parliaments*, 5th edn, London, 1993; and P. W. Hasler (ed.), *The House of Commons, 1558–1603*, 3 vols., Cheltenham, 1996.

On foreign policy, domestic and religious themes intermingle and personalities such as Mary Queen of Scots, the duke of Anjou, Spanish ambassadors like de Spes and da Silva, and the queen's ministers, especially Burghley, Walsingham and Leicester, are highlighted. The role of the notable Elizabethan sea-dogs, Ralegh, Frobisher, Gilbert, Drake and Hawkins has an impact on foreign relations. For an overview of foreign policy, see R. B. Wernham, *Before the Armada: the growth of English foreign policy 1485–1588*, London, 1966; and *The making of Elizabethan foreign policy 1558–1603*, California, 1980. For a brief analysis and a collection of documents, see S. Doran, *England and Europe 1485–1603*, London, 1986.

For Scotland, see Gordon Donaldson, *The Scottish Reformation*, Cambridge, 1960.

For Wales, see P. Williams, *The Council in the Marches of Wales under Elizabeth*, Cardiff, 1958; and G. Williams, *Welsh Reformation essays*, Cardiff, 1967.

For Ireland, see N. Canny, *The Elizabethan conquest of Ireland: A pattern established, 1565–1576*, Hassocks, 1976; B. Bradshaw, *The Irish constitutional revolution of the sixteenth century*, Cambridge, 1979; C. Brady, *The chief governors; the rise and fall of reform government in Tudor Ireland, 1536–1588*, Cambridge, 1994; and M. MacCarthy-Morrough, *The Munster plantation*, Oxford, 1986.

Elizabeth I: the later years, 1588–1603

Commemorative works on the Armada grew apace in 1988 and for a useful survey of that literature, see Simon Adams, 'The Grand Armada: 1988 and after', in *History*, Vol. 76 (1991); and note especially, F. Fernandez-Armesto, *The Spanish Armada*, Oxford, 1988; C. Martin and

Select bibliography

G. Parker, *The Spanish Armada*, London, 1988; M. J. Rodriguez-Salgado (ed.), *Armada*, Harmondsworth, 1988; R. Whiting, *The Enterprise of England*, Cheltenham, 1997; and R. B. Wernham, *The return of the Armada*, Oxford, 1994. For the impact of the Irish Nine Years' War on England in the 1590s, see John McGurk, *The Elizabethan conquest of Ireland*, Manchester, 1997.

The history of the puritan opposition has been revolutionised by the works of Patrick Collinson. In addition to those works already mentioned, see his biography of *Archbishop Grindal*, London, 1979; and essays in his *Godly people*, London, 1983. But also, see P. Lake, *Moderate puritans and the Elizabethan church*, Cambridge, 1983.

Local government and administration commands an enormous literature. For institutions. see G. R. Elton, *The Tudor constitution*, Cambridge, 2nd edn, 1982; and C. Coleman and D. Starkey (eds.), *Revolution reassessed: revisions in the history of Tudor government and administration*, Oxford, 1986.

For an overview of social and economic policies, see J. A. Sharpe, *Early modern England: A social history 1550–1760*, London, 1987. For a comprehensive survey of social and economic history in the reign, see D. Palliser, *The age of Elizabeth*, London, 1983; and K. Wrightson, *English society, 1580–1680*, London, 1995.

On the court and the cult of Gloriana, see R, Strong, *The cult of Elizabeth: Elizabethan portraiture and pageantry*, London, 1987; and his *Gloriana: the portraits of Queen Elizabeth I*, London, 1987; and also, A. Young, *Tudor and Jacobean tournaments*, London, 1987. J. N. King, *Tudor royal iconography: literature and art in an age of religious crisis*, Princeton, 1990, is a mine of information on how the Tudor dynasty as a whole projected its image. See also S. Doran, *Monarchy and matrimony – the courtships of Elizabeth I*, London, 1995. M. Aston, *The king's bedpost: reformation and iconography in a Tudor group portrait*, Cambridge, 1993, is noteworthy for its investigation into the images of Henry VIII and Edward VI. See also F. A. Yates, *Astraea; the imperial theme in the sixteenth century*, Harmondsworth, 1978; and D. M. Loades, *The Tudor court*, London, 1986. But for two views of popular culture, see F. Laroque, *Shakespeare's festive world*, tr. J. Lloyd, Cambridge, 1991; and Keith Thomas, *Religion and the decline of magic*, Harmondsworth, 1991.

Chronology

1455 *22 May:* The first battle of the Wars of the Roses is fought at St Albans.

1461 *29 March:* Edward IV defeats Henry VI at Towton.
28 June: Edward IV is crowned king.

1466 Louis XI of France allies with the earl of Warwick.

1469 *26 July:* Warwick defeats Edward IV at Edgecote.

1470 Edward IV flees to Flanders. Warwick restores Henry VI.

1471 *14 April:* Warwick is defeated and killed by Edward IV at Barnet.
4 May: Edward IV defeats Queen Margaret at Tewkesbury.
21 May: Edward enters London. King Henry VI is stabbed to death at the Tower of London.

1483 Edward IV dies and is succeeded by Edward V.
June: Richard, duke of Gloucester usurps the throne.
July: Edward V and his brother Richard – the Princes in the Tower – are murdered.

1485 *7 August:* Henry, duke of Richmond, lands at Milford Haven.
22 August: Richard III is defeated and killed at Bosworth.
7 November: Henry VII is crowned.

1486 Henry VII marries Elizabeth of York.

1487 *24 May:* The pretender, Lambert Simnel, is crowned in Dublin.
16 June: Simnel and his supporters are defeated at Stoke, near Newark in Nottinghamshire.

1488 *11 June:* James III of Scotland is murdered and succeeded by James IV.
October: A truce is made between England and Scotland.
The Treaty of Medina del Campo is signed between England and Spain.

1492 The treaty of Etaples is signed between England and France.
France abandons the pretender, Perkin Warbeck.

1494 Poynings' Law makes Irish legislation dependent on the prior consent of the king of England, confirmed by letters bearing his seal.

1495 Perkin Warbeck, supported by the Emperor Maximilian, fails to land at Deal, but flees to Scotland.

1496 England joins the Holy League against France.
Philip of Burgundy and Henry VII sign the *Magnus Intercursus*.
September: The Scots invade England.

1497 *July to September:* Perkin Warbeck lands in Cornwall, his forces are defeated and he is captured.
A truce is made with Scotland.

1499 Warbeck and Edward, earl of Warwick, are beheaded.

1502 *8 August:* James IV of Scotland marries Margaret Tudor, daughter of Henry VII.

1509 Henry VII dies and is succeeded by Henry VIII.
Henry marries his brother's widow, Catherine of Aragon.

1510 *17 August:* Empson and Dudley, Henry VII's tax collectors, are executed.

1513 *9 September:* The Scots and their French allies are defeated at Flodden. James IV is killed and is succeeded by James V.
The English defeat the French at 'The Battle of the Spurs'.

1514 Henry VIII makes peace with France.

1516 Thomas More's *Utopia* is published.

1519 Henry VIII and Francis I of France are among the candidates for the Imperial crown but Charles V, king of Spain, is elected Holy Roman Emperor.

1520 Henry VIII and Francis I meet at the Field of the Cloth of Gold.

1521 Henry VIII's book, *In defence of the seven sacraments*, is published. The pope rewards him with the title *Defensor Fidei* (Defender of the Faith).

1526–29 Negotiations take place with Rome about Henry VIII's divorce from Catherine of Aragon.

1529–36 Henry VIII's Reformation Parliaments meet.

1532 *May:* The Act of Submission of the English clergy is passed.
Thomas Cromwell becomes Henry's chief minister.

1533 *January:* Henry VIII marries Anne Boleyn in secret.
February: Thomas Cranmer becomes Archbishop of Canterbury.
Cranmer's court at Dunstable declares Henry VIII's marriage to Catherine void.
The Act of Restraint of Appeals is passed.

1534 The Act of Supremacy ending papal jurisdiction in England becomes law.
The Treasons Act is passed.

1535 *21 January:* Visitations of monasteries and churches are ordered.
22 June: Bishop John Fisher of Rochester is beheaded.
6 July: Thomas More is beheaded.

1536 The Act for the Dissolution of the Lesser Monasteries is passed.
The Pilgrimage of Grace takes place.
19 May: Anne Boleyn is beheaded.
30 May: Henry VIII marries Jane Seymour.

1537 Coverdale's 1535 translation of *The English Bible* is authorised.
24 October: Jane Seymour dies.

1539 The Six Articles Act re-affirms conservative doctrines.
The Act for the Dissolution of the Greater Monasteries is passed.

1540 *6 January:* Henry VIII marries Anne of Cleves.
6 July: The marriage is declared void.
28 July: Henry VIII marries Catherine Howard.

1541 Ireland is declared a kingdom and annexed to the crown of England.

1542 Sir Antony St Leger promotes the policy of 'Surrender and Regrant' in Ireland.
13 February: Catherine Howard is beheaded for adultery.
24 November: The Scots invade England and are defeated at Solway Moss.
8 December: Mary Queen of Scots is born.

1543 Treaty of Greenwich, ending the war between England and Scotland, is negotiated but is repudiated by the Scottish parliament.
May: The necessary doctrine of any Christian man (The King's book) is published.
12 July: Henry VIII marries Catherine Parr.

1544 The Third Succession Act is passed.
The English invade Scotland and attack Leith and Edinburgh.
14 September: Henry VIII takes Boulogne and it remains in English hands for eight years.

1547 Henry VIII dies and is succeeded by Edward VI.
The duke of Somerset is appointed Lord Protector.
The Act for the Dissolution of Chantries, Guilds and Colleges is passed.
September: The Scots are defeated at the Battle of Pinkie.

1549 The Act of Uniformity imposes the first Prayer Book of Edward VI.
Rebellion breaks out in Cornwall, and in East Anglia under Robert Kett.

1550 Somerset is deposed and succeeded by Northumberland.

1552 *January:* Somerset is executed on the orders of Northumberland.
The second Edwardian Prayer Book is issued.

1553 Edward VI dies and is succeeded by Mary I. The repeal of Edwardian religious legislation begins and the Mass is restored.
25 July: Mary I marries Philip, later Philip II of Spain.
August: Northumberland is executed on Tower Hill.

1554 *January:* Wyatt's Rebellion breaks out.
February: Lady Jane Grey is executed.

1555 The Act to restore papal supremacy becomes law.
The law *De heretico comburendo* is revived.
The burning of Protestant 'heretics' begins.

1556 Archbishop Cranmer is burnt at the stake.

1557 The Anglo-French War leads to the loss of Calais.

1558 *24 April:* Mary Queen of Scots marries Francis, the dauphin of France.
17 November: Mary I dies and is succeeded by Elizabeth I.

1559 The Peace of Cateau-Cambrésis is signed between England, France and Spain.
The Acts of Supremacy and Uniformity are restored once more, ending papal influence in England. A new Prayer Book is issued.
The Catholic bishops are removed.

1560 The Treaty of Edinburgh is signed between England and Scotland. An English force compels the withdrawal of French troops from Scotland.

1561 Mary Queen of Scots lands in Scotland.
The Wars of Religion begin in France.
Elizabeth I makes a treaty at Hampton Court with the Huguenots.

1563 Convocation approves the Thirty-nine Articles.

The first edition of John Foxe's *Actes and monuments* (or Book of martyrs) is published.

1564 A trade war breaks out between England and Spain over embargoes.

1565 *29 July:* Mary Queen of Scots marries Henry Darnley.

1567 *10 February:* Darnley is murdered. Civil war breaks out.

15 May: Mary Queen of Scots marries James Bothwell.

Mary is forced to abdicate as Queen of Scots.

1568 *19 May:* Mary is defeated in Scotland and escapes to England.

William Allen founds his seminary to train Catholic missionary priests in Douai.

1569 The first Desmond War breaks out in Ireland and lasts until 1573.

The northern earls rise up against Elizabeth I.

1570 *25 February:* The papal bull, *Regnans in excelsis*, excommunicates Elizabeth I and calls upon her subjects to overthrow her.

The English plantation of East Ulster is completed.

1571–72 *The first and second admonitions to parliament* are published by the puritans.

The Ridolfi plot to depose Elizabeth I is uncovered.

1575 Elizabeth I declines the sovereignty of the Netherlands.

1579 The second Desmond War begins in Ireland and is suppressed by 1583.

The privileges granted to Hansa merchants in England are withdrawn.

1580 The Jesuit mission arrives in England.

1581 Marriage negotiations begin between Francis, duke of Anjou, and Elizabeth I.

Recusancy fines are increased to £20 a month.

Edward Campion is arrested and is sentenced to be hung in London.

1583 The Throckmorton plot is discovered.

1584 The plantation of Munster begins and is completed by 1589.

1585 All Catholic priests are ordered to leave the realm within 40 days.

December: English troops under the earl of Leicester support the Dutch.

1586 Mary Queen of Scots is implicated in the Babington Conspiracy.

14–15 October: The trial of Mary Queen of Scots takes place.

1587 8 February: Mary Queen of Scots is beheaded at Fotheringhay.

1 March: Peter Wentworth MP challenges Elizabeth I's absolutism in church affairs.

August: Leicester returns to England after the failure of the Dutch expedition.

1588 *31 July–8 August:* The Spanish Armada is defeated.

The Welsh translation of *The Bible* by William Morgan appears.

The first of Shakespeare's plays is staged. (The last is staged in 1613.)

1590 The first part of Edmund Spenser's *Faerie queen* is published (completed 1596).

1592 Trinity College, Dublin is founded to train Protestant clergy.

1593 February: Parliament passes an Act against 'seditious sectaries and disloyal persons'.

John Greenwood, Henry Barrow and John Penry, opponents of royal supremacy, are executed.

Richard Hooker's *On the laws of ecclesiastical polity* is published.

1594   Hugh O'Neill, the earl of Tyrone, rebels and the Nine Years' War begins in Ireland.

1596   *April:* The Spanish sack Calais: the English sack Cadiz.

1597   Spanish naval expeditions against England fail.

1598   O'Neill is successful in Ireland, notably at 'The Yellow Ford', in August.
Lord Burghley, Elizabeth I's chief minister, dies.
13 September: Philip II of Spain dies and is succeeded by Philip III.

1599   Essex is appointed Lord Deputy of Ireland and makes an unfavourable treaty with O'Neill.
James VI of Scotland condemns Presbyterianism and asserts the Divine Right of Kings in his *Basilikon Doron*.

1600   Lord Mountjoy is appointed Lord Deputy of Ireland to prosecute the war against O'Neill.

1601   *25 February:* Essex is executed for attempted rebellion.
September: Spanish troops land at Kinsale.
24 December: At the Siege and Battle of Kinsale, Irish and Spanish forces are defeated. O'Neill withdraws to Ulster to continue the war.

1602   *2 January:* Spaniards surrender to Mountjoy.

1603   *20 March:* O'Neill submits at Mellifont to Mountjoy.
24 March: Elizabeth I dies and is succeeded by James VI of Scotland who is proclaimed James I of England, Scotland, Ireland and France.

Index

aristocracy *see* nobility
Arthur, prince of Wales, 25, 26, 30

Bacon, Francis, 23–4
Bacon, Sir Nicholas, 10
barons, *see* nobility
Beaufort, Margaret, countess of Richmond, 18, 19, 23, 26
Black Prince, the, 14
Boleyn, Anne, 37, 40, 42
Bosworth Field, Battle of (1485), 14, 19, 20, 23, 26

Camden, William, 21, 98
Campion, Edmund, 77–8, 95
Catherine of Aragon, 26–7, 33, 36–7, 38, 40, 43, 61
Catholicism: and Elizabeth I, 70, 72, 73, 74–5, 76–8, 82, 87; Mary Tudor's attempts to restore, 59–60, 61, 63–4, 66, 68, 71
Cecil, Sir Robert, 89, 93, 95
Cecil, William (later Lord Burghley), 50, 82, 88; and foreign policy, 78, 80; and religious policy, 71, 72, 73, 75, 76, 77
Chancery, 3–4
Charles I, King, 1
Charles V, Emperor, 36, 37, 44, 55, 61
Charles VIII, king of France, 26, 27
commonweal, 1, 3, 5, 14, 34
coronation ceremonies, 1–2, 9; Elizabeth I, 81
council (king's), 4–6, 20, 23, 34
Council in the Marches of Wales, 5, 25, 34, 109
Council of the North, 5, 25, 26, 34, 89, 109
Courtenay, Edward, 62, 63
Cranmer, Thomas, archbishop of Canterbury, 37–8, 41, 51, 53, 61, 64, 72; and the Elizabethan religious settlement, 72, 73
Cromwell, Thomas, 5, 37, 39, 40, 41, 43, 108

Davies, R. R., 25
de la Mare, Peter, 7
Dudley, Edmund, 24

Edward I, King, 6, 14, 43
Edward II, King, 6
Edward III, King, 6–7, 10, 14, 19

Edward IV, King, 15–17, 18, 62, 96, 111; appearance and character, 20; and the council, 6; and the Council of the North, 26; death, 17, 20; and finance, 4, 17, 50, 54, 56–7; and Henry VII, 23, 24, 25, 106
Edward V, King, 17, 18, 106
Edward VI, King, 40, 49–58, 61; abilities, 55; death, 54; health, 56; and Northumberland's rule, 52, 53–5; and the Somerset Protectorate, 49–52
Edwards, J. G., 8
Elizabeth I, Queen, 52, 70–105, 110–11; and the Armada, 78, 80, 81, 87–8, 91, 101–2, 110; birth, 40; character, 70–1, 101, 103; cult of, 2, 98–101; death, 95; and the economy, 88–9, 101; foreign policy, 78–80, 88, 110; and Ireland, 78, 83–4, 88, 93, 94, 101, 103, 110; local government and administration, 95–8; and Mary, Queen of Scots, 72, 75–6, 80, 81, 87, 91, 111; and Mary Tudor, 60, 64, 68; and the Northern Rebellion (1569), 75–7, 83, 109; and parliament, 89, 90–4, 101, 108; portraits of, 99; and religion, 70, 71–8, 81–3; royal progresses, 99, 109; and Scotland, 46; and the succession, 49, 53, 54, 70, 95; Tilbury speech, 98, 102; and the Wyatt Rebellion, 62, 63
Elizabeth of York, 18, 29
Empson, Sir Richard, 24, 25, 26
Essex, Robert Devereux, earl of, 88, 90, 94–5
Exchequer, 4

finances: and Edward IV, 4, 17, 50, 54, 56–7; and Elizabeth I, 89, 93; and the Exchequer, 4; and Henry VII, 4, 23, 24, 25, 29, 30, 50; and Henry VIII, 50; in the reign of Edward VI, 50, 54, 56–7; and Richard III, 4, 18
Flodden Field, Battle of (1513), 36, 44, 45
Fortescue, Sir John, 2, 8–9
Foxe, John, 66; *Book of martyrs*, 64
France: and Elizabeth I, 87, 88; and Henry VII, 26, 27; and Henry VIII, 36; and Mary, Queen of Scots, 45–6; and the Wyatt Rebellion, 62–3
Francis I, king of France, 36, 44

Gardiner, Stephen, bishop of Winchester (later Lord Chancellor), 51, 59, 62, 63, 66–7

Gresham, Sir Thomas, 56–7
Grey, Lady Jane, 52, 54, 59, 60, 63

Hampton Court Palace, 34–5, 37
Henry Fitzroy, duke of Richmond, 43, 110
Henry III, King, 4–5
Henry IV, King, 6, 7
Henry V, King, 6
Henry VI, King, 6, 14, 15, 16, 17, 23, 106
Henry VII, King, 14, 22–31, 29, 94;
    achievements, 29, 106–7; appearance, 23;
    and the Battle of Bosworth (1485), 19, 20,
    23; character and abilities, 23–4, 29; claim
    to the throne, 18–19; and the council, 20,
    23; and finance, 4, 23, 24, 25, 29, 30, 50;
    and foreign affairs, 26–7; and Ireland, 23,
    27–8, 110; and law and order, 24, 25, 26;
    and the nobility, 24, 26, 30–1; and the
    North, 25, 26; and parliament, 25, 108;
    portrait, 22; and trade, 27, 29; and Wales,
    23, 25, 30
Henry VIII, King, 32–48; achievements, 47;
    appearance and accomplishments, 46; and
    Cardinal Wolsey, 33, 34–7; and Catherine of
    Aragon, 27, 33, 36–7, 38, 40, 43, 61;
    character, 33; court, 46–7; death, 49; and
    finance, 50; and foreign policy, 35–7; and
    Ireland, 42–4, 110; last will and testament,
    49; and law and order, 41–2; marriages, 33,
    38, 40–1; and the office of Secretary, 4; and
    parliament, 8; personal possessions, 47;
    portrait, 32; and the Reformation, 37–41;
    and Scotland, 36, 44–6, 111; and Somerset,
    49; and Wales, 41–2
Hooker, Richard, 72, 94
Howard, Thomas, earl of Surrey (later duke of
    Norfolk), 42, 43

Ireland: and the Act of Union, 109; and
    Elizabeth I, 78, 83–4, 88, 93, 94, 101, 103,
    110; and Henry VII, 23, 27–8, 110; and Henry
    VIII, 42–4, 110; a Spaniard's account of, 102

James IV, king of Scotland, 24, 27, 36, 44
James V, king of Scotland, 44–5
James VI and I, King, 27, 70, 89, 95, 110, 111
John of Gaunt, 7, 23
justices of the peace, 95, 96–7

Kett rebellion (1549), 51, 55–6
Kildare, earls of (Fitzgeralds), 27–8, 42, 43,
    110
king's council, 4–6, 20, 23, 34
Knox, John, 45, 76–7

Lancaster, House of, 12, 14, 18, 23
languages, in the British Isles, 109
Latimer, Hugh, 51–2, 56, 64
law, and the monarch, 1–3

law and order, 24, 25, 26, 35, 109
'Learned in the Law' court, 24
Leicester, Robert Dudley, earl of, 75, 78, 80,
    84, 87, 88
local government and administration, 5, 25,
    26, 34, 109; Elizabethan, 95–8
lords lieutenants, 95, 96, 97

Magnus Intercursus, 27
Margaret of Burgundy, 24
Margaret, Queen (wife of Henry VI), 15–16
Margaret Tudor, queen of Scotland, 27, 45, 46,
    49
Mary, Queen of Scots, 45–6, 49, 50; and
    Elizabeth I, 72, 75–6, 80; execution of, 81,
    87, 91, 111
Mary Tudor, Queen, 45, 59–69, 96; birth, 33;
    death, 46; Guildhall speech, 62, 67;
    marriage to Philip of Spain, 59, 60, 61–2,
    63, 64; and the monasteries, 40; religious
    policies, 59–60, 61, 63–4, 66, 68; and the
    succession, 49, 53–4, 59–60; and the Wyatt
    Rebellion, 62–3, 67
Maximilian, Emperor, 27
Merciless Parliament (1388), 7
Middle Ages: background to the Tudors, 14–21;
    and the Exchequer, 4; and parliament, 6–7,
    8; and royal power, 1, 2; and the sealed writ,
    3–4
middle classes, 25, 90
mixed government, theory of, 10
monarchy, 1–13, 107; and the centralisation of
    authority, 108–9; and the coronation rites,
    1–2, 9; and the Exchequer, 4; and hereditary
    right, 1, 8; and the king's council, 4–6; and
    the law, 1–3, 14; and parliament, 5, 6–8, 10,
    14, 107–8; and the rise of bureaucracy, 1,
    3–6; and royal power, 1, 8–9, 10, 14, 98
monasteries, dissolution of the, 40, 53
More, Sir Thomas, 20, 38, 39, 46, 53, 61

Netherlands, and Elizabeth I, 76, 78–80, 84,
    87, 88, 110
nobility: barons, 3, 4; and Cardinal Wolsey,
    35; and the Council of the North, 26; and
    the earls of Kildare, 28; in Elizabethan
    England, 90; and the king's council, 5;
    overpowerful, 107, 109; and Parliament, 7;
    Scottish, 44; and the Wars of the Roses, 14,
    16, 17, 19
Northern Rebellion (1569), 75–7, 83, 109
Northumberland, John Dudley, duke of, 52,
    53–5, 59, 60, 61

Oxford Reformers, 33–4

Paget, William, 49, 50
Parker, Matthew, archbishop of Canterbury, 71,
    72, 73

parliament, 5, 6–8, 10, 14, 107–8; and Cardinal
    Wolsey, 34, 37; and Elizabeth I, 89, 90–4,
    101, 108; and Henry VII, 25, 108; and Henry
    VIII, 47; and Mary Tudor, 61; and
    Northumberland's rule, 53; Reformation,
    39; and the Yorkist dynasty, 15
Pavia, Battle of (1525), 36
Peasants' Revolt (1381), 7, 40
Philip of Burgundy, 27
Philip II, king of Spain: and the Armada, 80, 81,
    87–8; and Elizabeth I, 70, 73, 75, 78–80;
    marriage to Mary Tudor, 59, 60, 61–2, 63,
    64, 68
Pilgrimage of Grace, 40
Pinkie, Battle of (1547), 50, 53
Pole, Cardinal Reginald, 63, 66–7, 71
Poor Law (Elizabethan), 97
population, in Elizabethan England, 90, 103
Poynings, Sir Edward, 28
privy council, 5, 71, 90; and local government,
    96, 97
Protestantism: under Edward VI, 50–1, 53, 71,
    72; and Elizabeth I, 71–4, 88; and the
    Reformation, 34, 37–41, 42, 44
Puritans, and Elizabeth I, 73–4, 82, 83, 94

Reformation, 34, 37–41, 42, 44
religion: and Elizabeth I, 70, 71–8, 81–3; and
    Mary Tudor, 53–4, 59–60, 61, 63–4, 66, 68;
    and Renaissance England, 33–4; and the
    Somerset Protectorate, 50–1; see also
    Catholicism; Protestantism
Renaissance England, 33–4
Renard, Simon (Spanish ambassador), 60, 63,
    68
Richard II, King, 1, 6, 7, 9, 14
Richard III, King, 17–19, 20–1, 24, 106, 107;
    character, 20, 21; and the Council of the
    North, 26; finances, 4, 18
Roman Catholicism, see Catholicism

St Albans, Battle of (1455), 14, 15
Scotland, 27, 110–11; and the Act of Union,
    109; and Elizabeth I, 46; and Henry VIII, 36,
    44–6, 111; Somerset's invasion of, 50, 52,
    53
sealed writs, 3–4

Secretary, office of King's, 4
Seymour, Thomas, Lord High Admiral, 52
Shakespeare, William, 1, 9, 101
sheriffs, 95–6
Simnel, Lambert, 24
Smith, Thomas, 50
Somerset, Edmund Beaufort, duke of, 15
Somerset, Edward Seymour, duke of, 49–52,
    111
Spain: Treaty of Medina del Campo (1489),
    26–7; and Wolsey's foreign policy, 26; see
    also Philip II, king of Spain
Spenser, Edmund, 99
Star Chamber, 5, 24, 34, 35

taxes: and Cardinal Wolsey, 34; and Edward
    IV, 17; and Elizabeth I, 89, 93; and Henry
    VII, 24, 29; income tax, 4; and Mary Tudor,
    61; and parliament, 6–7, 10; poll tax, 4; and
    royal power, 2
trade: and Elizabeth I, 89, 90; and Henry VII,
    27; and Northumberland, 54–5; and
    Somerset, 50
Tudor despotism, 108
Tudor, Owen, 18–19

Vergil, Polydore, 19–20, 23, 29, 30

Wales, 23, 25, 30, 41–2, 109
Warbeck, Perkin, 24, 28
Wars of the Roses, 14, 15–16, 17, 18–21, 106–7
Warwick, John Dudley, earl of, see
    Northumberland
Warwick, Richard Neville, earl of, 5, 15, 16
Wentworth, Peter, 73, 89, 91
Westminster Palace, 6
Whitgift, Archbishop, 74, 82, 94
Wilkinson, B., 8
Wolsey, Cardinal Thomas, 21, 33, 34–7, 39,
    40, 42; dismissal and death, 37; and foreign
    policy, 35–7
Woodville, Elizabeth, 16, 23–4
writs: and parliament, 6; sealed, 3–4
Wyatt Rebellion, 62–3, 67
Wycliffe, John, 2, 39

Yorkist dynasty, 6, 13, 14, 15–17, 23, 106–7